HAPPILY

EVER

AFTER

HAPPILY

EVER

AFTER

Retirement doesn't have to be just a fairy tale

JIM BLACK

Published by Advantage, Charleston, South Carolina.
Member of Advantage Media Group.

ADVANTAGE is a registered trademark and the Advantage colophon is a trademark of Advantage Media Group, Inc.

Printed in the United States of America.

ISBN: 978-159932-305-3
LCCN: 2012939152

This publication is designed to provide accurate and authoritative information in regard to the subject matter covered. It is sold with the understanding that the publisher is not engaged in rendering legal, accounting, or other professional services. If legal advice or other expert assistance is required, the services of a competent professional person should be sought.

Advantage Media Group is proud to be a part of the Tree Neutral® program. Tree Neutral offsets the number of trees consumed in the production and printing of this book by taking proactive steps such as planting trees in direct proportion to the number of trees used to print books. To learn more about Tree Neutral, please visit www.treeneutral.com. To learn more about Advantage's commitment to being a responsible steward of the environment, please visit www.advantagefamily.com/green

Advantage Media Group is a leading publisher of business, motivation, and self-help authors. Do you have a manuscript or book idea that you would like to have considered for publication? Please visit www.amgbook.com or call 1.866.775.1696

I wish to dedicate this book to my beautiful and patient wife who has stuck with me for the last 24 years. Ann, you have made everything else I do worthwhile. Your disposition and confidence has made my life a joy.

I would also like to thank my children: Jessica, Tyler, Zach, Josh, Kendra, and Charlotte who together made me realize the importance of planning for retirement. Spending money on my children gave me a crash course in understanding the need to plan for the future.

I realized that with six children, I either needed to win the lottery, have one of my children become a professional athlete, or start making plans and saving money today for the phase of life when my time becomes my own.

It is that insight that has allowed me to understand and help so many clients enjoy the retirement, the income and the freedom that they wished for…to truly be a part of their Happily Ever After.

CONTENTS

Off on the Right Foot

INVESTMENTS AND
FINANCIAL PLANNING

**"Explain to me again why enjoying life when I retire
is more important than enjoying life now."**

Once upon a time… there was a gentleman preparing to retire. He'd done well in running a small business and now, in his mid-seventies, he came to our office to work out the details of retirement. We began to chat about his finances.

"I love Starbucks stock, you'll notice," he said at one point.

I had noticed. About 90 percent of his total assets were tied up in Starbucks stock – a dangerous concentration in a single stock, no matter what it is.

Nonetheless, at the time, Starbucks was still a pretty good position: It was at $27 per share, and his average cost of purchase was only about $12 per share.

"You're in great shape," I ventured to say. "You can make $15 a share on every one of those that you sell." I gave him some ideas about how he could reallocate much of that Starbucks stock so that he could derive a monthly income from it. At the time, Starbucks wasn't paying dividends, and he would need to develop income sources if he were to retire.

"Look," he responded, "I just can't sell my Starbucks stock right now. I'd be losing money."

"Losing money?" I asked, tilting my head. "Help me understand how you'd lose money."

"Well," he explained, "the stock has been as high as $40 a share. If I sell it at $27 a share, I'm losing $13 a share. I love your suggestions, but first I'm going to hold off till Starbucks gets back up to $40. Then I'll go ahead with my retirement and I'll make those adjustments you're talking about, okay?"

He was adamant that Starbucks wouldn't let him down. However, if you track what happened to Starbucks stock, you realize it went from that heady figure of $40 (back in 2006) down to $35, then to $27, and then down and down, closing under $8 in late 2008.

Meanwhile, as we know, the economy was tanking, and the gentleman's business was down 70 percent. To meet his payroll and keep his operations going, he had to sell assets – namely, Starbucks stock, as it was on its slide down.

The stock eventually recovered and even began paying dividends, but by then this client could not retire. He had had to sell too much. Had he only walked away when he had the money, he could have been free of his worries. At that point, retirement seemed to be a fading dream.

He was thinking the way people do when they are in accumulation mode. They see a gain as a loss of money that they could have or should have had.

During your working years, you are typically in such a mindset. "I'm saving my money for —" Just fill in the blank with whatever you're saving for someday. You are striving to make as much as you can toward that end. But the day you retire, and you get the last paycheck you ever expect for the rest of your life, you're no longer saving for someday. Someday has arrived.

It's a major change in life. People look forward to retiring. When they do, they rush to take a few trips, and then they don't know what to do with themselves. That's why I sit down with soon-to-retire clients and talk about such matters. Through retirement coaching, you can get a clearer picture of how you are going to spend your time and how each day will look as you set about fulfilling lifelong dreams.

We also talk about a crucial consideration: Will you have enough money to sustain you while you do those things? If you're still in the mode of accumulating, you can destroy the nest egg that you nurtured for so long. Things don't have to be that way.

Time for a new approach

When you get to retirement, the rules are totally different. Yet nobody's going to walk out with a rulebook and say, "Here's how you succeed in retirement." This doesn't happen.

Few people realize they need to change their approach to their investments in retirement. It's not until they get hit on the head a couple of times that they seem ready to make a change. It's unfortunate that for many it takes a loss before they realize what they're doing isn't working anymore.

Those who have money for retirement are the ones who were successful in accumulating and saving it – all those trips they didn't take, all that money saved for the long haul. Their strategies were successful. When the market went down, they waited for it to come up, or during those years they put money in growth investments and managed to succeed.

The reality is, however, that if they continue to do that in retirement, they will fail. What worked successfully for the first forty years of their lives is what kills them in retirement. "If this has worked great so far," they tell themselves, "why do anything differently?" So they don't – until things go badly for them. Some lose significant assets. That's when they start looking for another strategy.

When you're working, with twenty years to go until retirement, you typically have much of your assets in growth investments. You may even feel miffed or frustrated if an investment generates income because you don't need that income yet and you don't want to pay a tax on it.

However, once your salary ceases, the scenario flips around. You need income more than you need growth. The only reason you want growth in retirement is to make sure you have the income you will need and want for the rest of your life. Retirees often don't realize the change in emphasis, so they keep much of their money unnecessarily exposed in the market – to their peril.

That transition can be hard to make. It's thinking backwards from how you've done it successfully for decades. Typically, among couples, men take more risks and women are more conservative. The male approach can work well during accumulation years, but retirement calls for an increasingly female approach. Too often, however, the transition between approaches doesn't happen until something financially painful has happened.

In this book, I hope to help you understand when it is the appropriate time to move away from growth investments and begin developing a portfolio that produces an income. Planning for this should begin well before retirement. At retirement, you want to be positioned for protection from the market's whims because you no longer will have decades of investment life to recover from a big loss.

Sometimes, unfortunately, the very strategy upon which you thrived while employed can become the source of your downfall during retirement. Your income grew: it paid all your bills and enabled you to treat yourself well. You believed in it and in yourself, and you still do. But times change. Having all your assets in one place, no matter how successful it has been, becomes an unacceptable concentration of wealth.

Think of the buggy whip. Once everyone needed one, but no more. If a stubborn buggy-whip investor could have lived until today, he'd be a long-since broke investor. And remember the first cell phones, which were big as bricks? Compare those to today's smartphones. Once everybody wanted a personal organizer, but there's little demand for those as today's smartphones proliferate. Something else could come along and turn these smartphones into yesterday's toys.

Once, people flocked to the picture shows. Then they began staying home, watching movies they rented at video stores. Then, people began downloading movies. The rental giant Blockbuster filed for bankruptcy. Hollywood Video is gone.

As times change, fortunes change too. If you sink all your money into one investment, industry, or sector, without regard for economic and societal trends, you are risking big trouble. If you think the sun will shine forever on your favorite investment, think twice.

The lesson for those anticipating retirement – and that means most of us – is to diversify your investments. In retirement, you will need certain assets right away for income, while others can be left to grow, for the time being, so they can produce income a decade or two down the road.

Getting off on the right foot

When my son Zach was a toddler, it took him a while to learn to put on his own shoes. After he'd put considerable effort into it one day, I noticed something wasn't quite right.

"Zach," I said, "your shoes are on the wrong feet."

He looked down, concerned, then smiled.

"Oh, Dad, stop teasing! These are the only feet I have."

Zach's comment surprised me. His interpretation would never have occurred to me. But each of us had a point. We each had a different way of looking at the same situation.

I think of Zach's comment whenever clients tell me they're making such risky investments in retirement because it's the only way to ensure sufficient income for the rest of their lives. I can offer another way of looking at it: By taking so much risk, they likely won't ensure that income.

Highly aggressive investments can be akin to outright gambling. The better strategy is to go for the gain while avoiding the risks. It can be done – if you play by a different set of rules than those you've long been accustomed to following.

Imagine yourself at a Las Vegas blackjack table. You put $10 down on the table. If you win, you have a total of $20, but if you lose, you have zero. Your risk is 100 percent: You either double your money or you lose it. Now, suppose there is a different set of rules: If you win, you only get $6, for a total of $16. However, if you lose, you get to keep your $10 and play again.

By which set of rules would you rather play? Consider these questions: As an investor, if it had been possible for you to participate in the stock market's returns while avoiding its losses, how would your situation be different today? If you got the upside without a downside, would you be better off?

You don't hear much about such investment strategies. But they have existed for years.

It's crucial to keep an open mind during retirement planning. You have exciting years ahead and you want to get off on the right foot. That means attending to three fundamental retirement strategies: keeping your taxes down, keeping your income up, and managing your risks sensibly.

Minimizing taxes

Recently, when I was on a flight from Orlando, the flight attendant asked me a question that is becoming rare in the air: "Would you like a meal?"

"Well, what are my choices?" I asked her.

"Yes or no."

You might think of taxes that way, too. You either pay what's due or you risk going to jail. It's hardly a real choice. However, how much is due and how much you pay is another matter. You can do much to reduce that tax hit.

Untamed taxes can take a significant bite out of your retirement income. Instead, imagine that you could cut your tax bill from $10,000 to $5,000 through effective tax planning. You would be getting quite a nice rate of return for your effort. In seminars, I sometimes ask people what rate of return they think that would be.

"Two hundred percent," one man once responded.

"How so?" I asked.

"Well, that's five grand that I don't pay to Uncle Sam anymore. And that's an extra five grand that I get to use for myself."

His math is a bit suspect, but I like the attitude.

The issue of taxes can become even more important during retirement than it is during one's working years. A retiree no longer gets many deductions: His or her house often is paid off, for example, so the mortgage interest deduction is gone. A retiree's Social Security income is taxed based on the amount of additional income: Some people pay no tax on their benefits, while others have to count 85 percent of their Social Security check as taxable income.

You probably know the fairy tale of Hansel and Gretel, lost in the woods until they find the witch's house. The old hag fattens them up as she prepares for the feast. Tax rules sometimes seem to treat retirees that way.

For example, six months after turning seventy, many retirees encounter the old lie about retirement accounts. They were told that their 401(k) or their IRA would be a great tax savings because upon retirement they'd be in a lower tax bracket and the government wouldn't consume so much of their nest eggs.

Now, retirees come to my office regularly, angry and frustrated, because, it turns out, they're in a higher tax bracket and yet must take a required minimum distribution annually. What they were told is not how it works out, and much of their retirement money is at stake. They feel as if they have been fattened for the government's feast.

Yet, with diligence in managing taxation, whether by tailoring your style of investments or planning efficiently for the distribution of your estate, you can keep the government's take to a minimum.

Maximizing income

A hundred years ago, wealth was defined by how much a person owned in assets. It was the age of the land grab and the amassed fortune – if you owned a railroad, you were wealthy. In time, people realized that wealth is not about owning assets; it's about what those assets do for their owners. Increasingly, in recent years, wealth has tended to be defined more as a matter of cash flow. The emphasis has turned to how much income wealth can generate, which is of particular concern to a retiree. No fortune makes you happy if you have no liquid cash with which to pay the bills.

For today's retirees, maximizing income comes down to arranging their finances so that they live the lifestyle they dreamed they would have at this stage of life. At retirement, you basically have all the assets you're ever going to have. The nuts you've stored away have to last the rest of your season, and if you lose a lot of that stash because of a mistake in the market or other financial dealings, you won't have what you need. I see men who look as if they're eighty working at McDonald's – and I'm guessing that was not their plan for retirement.

For some inexplicable reason, people have been told that when they retire they only need a fraction of whatever their income was prior to retirement. That's absolutely untrue. I have seen countless people whose income needs rise in retirement. Some retirees were actually so busy during their working years that they spent less than they do in retirement– or would like to spend.

Most retirement expenses are fixed. If you die, your surviving spouse's expenses will not suddenly fall by fifty percent. Your spouse's grocery bills may go down somewhat, and you won't be around any more to leave all those lights on, but that's minimal. The costs of living will stay much the same.

If you have the cash flow you need for your retirement expenses, many troubles go away. However, without that cash flow, retirement is a miserable time. A woman recently came to my office explaining that she had run out of money. She said she wished she were dead. It was painful to hear.

Her case was extreme, but many people fear a similar fate. Retirees with sufficient cash flow can eliminate that fear. They know they're prepared. They know enough money will be there for them. In this book, I share strategies with you for developing a retirement income so you too can find that peace of mind.

Managing risk

In the investment world, a traditional concept encourages people to distribute their money in a variety of places. That's the concept of asset allocation. You put some money in various types of equities, some in bonds, some in this, and some in that. If you set all the boats sailing, the concept goes, they cannot all sink at the same time.

"Let's reduce your risk," brokers or money managers tell retirees, and the idea seems to make sense. However, the problem is that when all investments within the portfolio are 100 percent vulnerable to some degree of risk, then they will remain 100 percent vulnerable to risk even if some of those investments become somewhat safer. In retirement, you certainly can and probably should have some money at risk. Yet you absolutely need to have some money (whether it's in a savings account, a CD, or an annuity) with a stated guarantee.

The traditional asset allocation model puts the entire portfolio at varying degrees of risk. I take a different approach: Instead of divvying up money by degree of risk, I emphasize designating it into sections, as either income money or growth money.

The income money shouldn't have any risk, because it is money that you're going to live on for the next five, ten, or fifteen years. The growth money, in contrast, is money that you know you won't need for a long time. You can invest that money as you would if you were in your forties again, because you can be confident you won't need it for another twenty years.

Even if you're not making much from your income money – and recently the percentages were getting down toward zero – you can be satisfied with that. Why? It's far more important to have that money there and available, even with low earnings, than to invest with risk and thus be exposed to big losses if the market were to fall by, say, 50 percent. In that case, your retirement funds would be ravaged, and you wouldn't have time to recover.

"You're called 'boomers' because 'boom' is the sound most of you will make when you crash into your retirement years."

Consequences of poor planning

It happens to so many retirees: They amble their way through life without devising any retirement plans. The consequences can be troubling – and sometimes tragic.

Consider this case from the New York State Supreme Court: A schoolteacher, married for twenty-seven years, neglected to name her husband as the beneficiary on their retirement account. She believed that no beneficiary had been named and that if she were to die, he would automatically get the money. When she did die, he didn't get the money. Beneficiaries had indeed been listed: she had designated her mother, uncle, and sister as beneficiaries before she married. The mother and uncle were dead, so the sister got a check for $900,000. What did she do with it? She kept every dime. She knew the couple had been happily married, but she kept it all. The bereaved husband took her all the way to the State Supreme Court but got nothing. The judges had little choice.

It could all have been avoided through simple planning.

Such estate disputes can drag on for years in court, as numerous cases among the wealthy and famous will attest. Marilyn Monroe, for example, died at age thirty-six, and it took forty-six years to resolve her estate.

For most retirees, however, lack of efficient planning mostly results not in tragedy but in a sense of unease, which can be remedied through good retirement coaching.

Charting the years ahead

The prospect of retirement can be daunting, but effective planning and good counseling can eliminate any fears. Knowing what to expect helps immensely. Knowing you will be all right financially gives you peace of mind.

Toward that end, an important part of the process is getting your documents in order. Often, we find that those important papers are in quite a sad state of disarray. We ask new clients to bring in documentation of all their assets, and as we go through these documents we invariably find that the clients have forgotten about a statement or something is missing, which they thought they had included.

The reason your retirement adviser needs a clear picture of your finances is so that together you can develop a portfolio and a strategy that will keep you set for the rest of your life.

With my clients, I use what I call the bucket strategy, which we'll discuss in greater detail in Chapter Four. The concept, in essence, is simple: Money withdrawn for income should come from a portfolio's lower-earning accounts. Most retirees, however, tap their higher-earning accounts, and that's backwards. Those accounts should remain untouched so that they can compound for later years.

Under the bucket strategy, the retiree's assets are categorized and, to start with, labeled Buckets A, B, and C.

Bucket A is what I call the distribution bucket. That's where we put the assets that will produce an income for the first five years of retirement. Virtually every retiree wants his or her investments to produce a monthly income, so we set that up. The money, which comes from a savings account or some other vehicle, goes regularly into the retiree's checking account. Bucket A is bound to have a low rate of return, but that's not important. What's important is that it be a liquid source of regular income during the first sixty months of retirement.

Meanwhile, we set up Bucket B, in which we place assets representing money the retiree knows he or she will not need for at least five years. These assets can be placed in investments that have better rates of return. Typically, a better return reduces liquidity, so the money in Bucket B is less readily available. Instead, it's allowed to grow untouched for five years.

After five years, when the money in Bucket A has all been withdrawn and spent, the money in Bucket B becomes available. Since it was allowed to grow for the first five years, it then becomes the new Bucket A for the next five years, or the retiree's new source of income.

Meanwhile, the retiree has other assets, which are initially labeled Bucket C. Initially, this bucket holds money the retiree won't need for ten years, which is invested for a still-higher rate of return. After five years, Bucket C becomes Bucket B; after another five years, it becomes Bucket A. All that money that has been compounding, untouched, then becomes available for income.

In this way, a retiree is able to spend all assets as income, yet the compounding of money not currently in use preserves the portfolio, so the assets still are there.

When beginning this strategy, we also set up what we call Bucket G. That's growth money. That's money at risk in the market. For the first twenty years, a retiree's income comes from fixed sources, so it's a long time before he or she needs money from Bucket G. So, if it's a bad year in the market – let's say the market goes down 50 percent – the retiree need not worry because the income is still secure and he or she has many years for the market to recover.

The people in retirement who get in trouble are the ones who, day by day, are looking at the stock market and determining what they're going to do, how much they're going to spend, and how they're going to live their lives simply by what happens to the market on a daily basis.

The beauty of the bucket system is that it reduces stress, even in uncertain times with wildly fluctuating markets. The only money you have at risk in such a market is money you won't need for a long time; this allows you to recoup any losses. It's the scenario of a young investor. Time can still work to your advantage, even in retirement.

Reducing stress is a major goal of good financial planning. When new clients come in for advice, they're often afraid they're going to run out of income. With this system, I can basically tell them – within reasonable parameters based on changing interest rates and other factors – how much income they can draw every month, all the way up to age one hundred.

I also build in an inflation factor, so that clients can see their income increasing through all those years. In reality, though, their expenses won't necessarily increase for all that time. The expenses will increase for several years, but then they will level off and, as the years advance, decrease. Nonetheless, I set up each client's income stream so that it increases yearly, reassuring him or her that it likely will be more than is needed. That provides added comfort, especially for those facing health concerns. It's reassuring to know some extra money will be there.

Who gets your money?

Another major aspect of financial planning for retirees is dealing with the estate. How much money will be left over to give to the kids and grandkids? Who gets how much, under what conditions? Estate planning requires careful assessment of who will be a responsible steward of the money you worked so hard to save for so many years. It calls for careful foresight and good judgment.

After all, you don't want to end up like poor Ernie and his dad.

In seminars, I tell Ernie's story. He was a bachelor who'd been helping his dad run the family business and recently had found out that, after his dad died, he'd inherit $20 million. His dad had been sickly lately, so Ernie decided to find a wife with whom he could share that fortune. He went to an investment club meeting, saw a beautiful woman, and got up the courage to talk to her.

"Hi, my name's Ernie," he said, "and when my sickly father dies, I'm going to inherit $20 million."

The beautiful woman raised an eyebrow, nodded, and took his card. Three days later, she became his stepmother.

People will be people. However, you can control how your estate is distributed. You can leave money, along with conditions, to your children. You can set up what is known as a dynasty trust, for example, which can protect your assets from creditors or from divorce claims indefinitely.

How do you think those big-name billionaires managed to maintain their family fortunes throughout a hundred years of philandering and divorces? It's because they had dynasty trusts. Historically, you had to have a hundred million dollars to set one up. The rules changed a decade or so ago and now regular folks can have them, too.

You can set up a trust that will protect your kids. Let's say you have a lousy, stinking, fill-in-the-blank son-in-law or daughter-in-law. You suspect he or she will soon be history. However, in a divorce from your child, that scoundrel will get half the inheritance you leave to that child. A dynasty trust will protect that asset virtually forever. In Washington, the term of protection is 150 years. In Utah, it's 1,000 years. In Nevada and Alaska, it's in perpetuity. Forever. A bazillion years, if you want.

I advised a client a number of years ago to set up a trust. I'm not saying trusts are for everyone, by any means. But his situation involved a second marriage and an estate worth hundreds of thousands of dollars. The situation seemed to call for a trust.

"It's no problem," he assured me. "Why, I've been married to this woman forty years now. She's raised my boy, my only son, since he was seven. She'll do what's right."

I talked to her after his death. "You know, I've been thinking," she said. "I'm just never going to be able to spend all that money in my lifetime. So, I tell you what: Let's split this up with my son right away."

"Right away" apparently wasn't soon enough. The son sued his stepmother for the whole estate. Now, she'd give the money to a stranger or throw it in the street before she'd give it to the son. The family has been ripped apart – all for my client's lack of taking an hour to do some simple planning.

Yes, I know: You think it won't happen in your family, right? But it happens.

Most retirees just want to distribute their money fairly among their children, or they want to know how to pass on money to charities efficiently. So, I tell clients to think of their assets as "live-on" money and "leave-on" money. Live-on money is the income they'll need for the rest of their lives. Leave-on money consists of assets that they may not need over the course of their lifetimes – and that's the category that calls for careful estate planning. Otherwise, the tax consequences can be severe, although they need not be so. I once heard it put like this: The only people who pay estate taxes are those who wanted to do so.

Retire on your terms

Retiring successfully means that you will have the income that you need and want for the rest of your life, regardless of what happens to interest and inflation rates, the stock market, or politics in Washington, D.C.

Above all, you want to retire on your terms. That means making sure you determine your lifestyle, regardless of those outside factors. They need not control you. You decide what you're going to do with your time – whether it's work, travel, or enjoying the grandkids. You have the freedom to do whatever you want to do with the rest of your life.

Baby boomers, many of whom are planning now for retirement, are unbelievably optimistic. They've seen some difficult situations, from war to inflation, but they tend to feel it's all going to work out. They are moving forward into their retirement years with the certainty that they can, indeed, live happily ever after.

Many Happy Returns

FINANCIAL PLANNING

"You found a dime on the sidewalk and didn't invest it.
Does this mean you've changed your mind about retiring someday?"

What is your biggest fear about retirement? In the 1980s, retirees answered a survey on this topic and indicated their biggest fear was dying. When they were asked the same question a few years ago, their biggest fear was that they would live too long – that is, that they would outlive their money.

Getting that last paycheck from your employer as you embark on retirement is a daunting prospect. The money you have saved is essentially what you will count on to maintain your desired lifestyle for the rest of your life. You're bound to be concerned that you might withdraw too much too soon.

How much can you safely withdraw from your savings during retirement so that you don't outlast your money? There's an art to figuring that out. When clients first come to see me, they seldom have any idea how to answer that question. They know their net worth. They know what their house is worth and how much they have in their retirement accounts. Yet few have a clue about how much income their assets can generate for them on an ongoing basis, especially if they factor in inflation and the unknown number of years that money must last.

Medical advances have upped the ante for retirement. You're less likely to die soon after retiring. In fact, you may live for decades – and those same medical advances mean you could face hefty healthcare bills. A retiree, then, knowing that he or she could live for quite some time, needs to do some planning for at least that long.

Once you retire you can't afford to make any more financial mistakes. If you do that and you run out of money, you'll be back in the working world for whatever pay you can command. To avoid that, you need more certainty that your nest egg won't crack.

Because of longer life expectancies, baby boomers retiring today could actually live for more retirement years than they did working years. They worked for thirty-five or forty years and could end up being in retirement for thirty-five or forty years – or longer. That's kind of a frightening concept, when you consider that perhaps you saved only a few percentage points every year of your total income, and now you have to make that little bit stretch for more years than the number you worked.

How much can you withdraw?

How much can you withdraw from your retirement funds each year? You'll find formulas designed to give you an idea, though they each have their drawbacks.

One is a concept called "Monte Carlo." It weighs how your investments have fared traditionally and, based on that calculation, projects whether you will run out of money. A Monte Carlo, if it's a good one, professes to offer you reassurance with 90 percent certainty. Now, imagine you are on a plane to London and the pilot announces, "We are experiencing relatively stable flight conditions with scattered storms, but we have a better than 90 percent chance of arriving safely in London. Have a nice flight." You get the picture.

Others will tell you that you should be just fine if you remove just 4 or 5 percent each year. But that depends on the economy. If you had a million dollars on January 1, 2000, and drew out just five percent per year, you would

have been broke after a decade. That's just one decade –
and it's likely you'll live a few more.

Brokerage companies and mutual fund companies
have a vested interest in persuading people not to play it
safe. If you go to one of their websites, you'll likely see a
retirement calculator demonstrating that if you invest in an
assortment of funds, chances are you can safely withdraw
four or five percent of your portfolio annually. You don't
get a lot of detail about that "chances are" concept. If a
down market occurs, you could find your portfolio down
50 percent rather than the market's 20 or 30 percent.

When withdrawing retirement money, the biggest
mistake you can make is to take it from an account that
rises and falls along with the market. I see this happen all
the time. In a good year, you might withdraw your money
and your account would seem none the worse for it. That's
one way to look at it.

Alternatively, you could consider that you forfeited the
opportunity to compound growth. You got a zero return
in an up market. Sad, but it could be worse. If you keep
taking withdrawals in a down market, your portfolio will
dwindle to the point where in a few years you'll be running
out of money – regardless of whether the market rebounds
or no.

Consider the cost of a loss: If the stock market falls
50 percent one year, then gains 50 percent the next, what
happens to an invested dollar? Do you break even? If you

do the math, you'll find you end up with 75 cents. To break even, you need to recover double what you lost, which is an unlikely scenario.

Strategies on three fronts

There's a better way to tap your money for retirement. In essence, use money that isn't subject to the market's volatility. Don't subject any money to risk unless you know you won't need it for years.

The number one goal my clients and I work together to reach is ensuring they will have enough money to last them throughout retirement, not just for their essentials but also for their dreams. That requires planning on three strategic fronts: taxation, income, and risk control.

Taming your taxes

Taxes, for one, must be tamed. The first consideration is cash flow: Every cent you pay in taxes is a cent that you're not getting for your own cash flow.

What are some things people can do that reduce their tax liability? For one, they can take all the deductions to which they are entitled. In addition, they should take advantage of tax credits. Deductions are good; credits are better. Credits go right against taxes on the bottom line – and there have been some good ones available, such as exemptions from long-term capital gains taxes, though many people are unfamiliar with them. Some credits are based on how much you spend, such as energy efficiency credits. Your financial and tax adviser can help you learn more. Remember, tax laws change every year, so what was available when this book was written may not still be an option when you read it. In contrast, there will probably be new options available for you when these expire.

Above all, remember this rule: Never, ever get into a situation in which you are paying taxes on interest and dividends that you do not spend. Don't do it. How do you know whether you're breaking that rule? It's simple. Look at your tax return. If there's an amount on lines 8 and 9 that you did not spend as income but reinvested instead, you are paying taxes on it unnecessarily. If your types of investments generate reportable income, the IRS will surely take its cut. The government – not you – reaps the benefits.

Many retirees understand that a portion of their Social Security income is subject to taxation, but they are unclear about how this works. Many retirees are intrigued by the words "tax-free investments," but if you receive Social Security and your income from those investments exceeds the tax-free threshold, you will be handing money over to the government.

Here's an example: Often, retirees are impressed by the tax-free nature of municipal bonds. It's true that earnings from municipal bonds are not subject to income tax.

However, those earnings are included in calculations to determine how much of a retiree's Social Security benefits will be taxed. An investment in so-called tax-free bonds actually becomes a tax liability in that manner. Since you shouldn't be paying income tax on money unless you're using it for income, instead you should invest that money elsewhere, in vehicles that don't generate taxable dividend interest.

Most people who come through my office also face estate tax issues. Recently, most people haven't faced an estate tax issue because there are exemptions on estates valued at less than $10 million. There aren't that many people who have estates over $10 million. However, these tax laws are all changing. In January 2013, that exemption is supposed to be reduced to $1 million. Remember, when you die, everything gets added up to determine the taxable consequences, including your home, your investments, and even your furnishings.

When it comes to passing assets on to the next generation, there is no worse asset on the planet than a retirement account, whether it's an IRA, 401(k), TSA, or 403(b), etc. In contrast, there's just about no better asset than a Roth IRA, which can work to your advantage. When you put money into a Roth, you pay income tax up front, not when you withdraw the money; then, all accumulations truly are tax-free, no matter how the Roth is invested. Your earnings from a Roth do not count against your Social

Security threshold either, so you suffer no penalty that way. Finally, because you've paid the taxes instead of deferring them, your loved ones will not inherit a huge tax liability along with the money. (We'll talk more about Roth IRAs, and how you might convert your assets to one, in Chapter Two.)

Often, a client will tell me something like this: "I want to make sure Little Jimmy gets x number of dollars." That's nice, I'll respond, but let's make sure that you have what you need first. It's important to take care of your own needs and dreams during your lifetime and to keep money for that separate from other funds. Then, when we look at what's going to go to the next generation, we can look at which assets will be the most tax-efficient to pass on, versus the ones that the government will hit hard with taxes.

Now and then I used to hear a client say that finding ways to avoid taxes is somehow unfair or unpatriotic. I'm not hearing that much anymore. It seems people feel just as patriotic paying half as much in taxes. The government intends tax exemptions to be used; government officials expect that you will take advantage of these exceptions and presume you will do what you can to pay as little as you ethically, morally, and legally can. If you don't do that, you have nobody to blame but yourself. You either have to acquire the knowledge or hire someone who has the knowledge and can put those tools to work for you.

Frankly, a prevailing feeling among my clients is irritation. They are irritated the government is wasting their money and feel it has no concept of how hard the citizens have worked for their pay. I don't think anybody feels guilty about reducing the tax bite anymore.

If you let the government tax you to the maximum, it will spend the money the way it wishes. You lose control. Those untold thousands of dollars that go to taxes unnecessarily could have gone to your charity (or charities) of choice instead. Cutting your tax bill doesn't mean you are forsaking your civic duty or don't have a giving heart. Rather, it allows you to decide how your charitable contributions will be directed.

A reliable income

It is absolutely possible, no matter what may come down the pike economically, to feel confident and secure. In helping my clients design their portfolios to provide them with lifetime incomes, I don't rely on what's happening out in the world to determine what we can and can't do. I throw out the typical asset allocation model that distributes money among various risk categories, some riskier than others. That model works well for people who are still employed, but retirees need a different approach – so I think of their money quite differently.

Because retirees, ordinarily, will no longer be drawing a paycheck, I separate their assets into income money and growth money, and handle those sets very differently. For income money, I use assets that are not exposed to any risk. In 2008, when the market was down 40 percent, not one of my clients who went through this planning process had to change his or her amount of income or cut back on lifestyle. I had identified the clients' income needs and set corresponding amounts aside in safe investments, with the principal guaranteed. The rate of return was lower, but that was the trade-off. Our clients could accept the lower rate because they had other assets – money they didn't need for a decade or two – out there in the market, prospering in good years while having enough time to recover in bad ones.

Did these clients lose money in the market? In 2008, they absolutely did. But these losses didn't change their lifestyle; like young investors, they'll have years to get back on track. They have ten or fifteen years for that money to recover before it becomes a real concern for them.

For many, the economic collapse of 2008 did wreak financial havoc. I know of a senior bank officer whose entire portfolio was devoted to Washington Mutual. "It's a great bank," the officer had said, citing a long career there and loyalty to coworkers. Then that great bank went bankrupt. Multimillions in company stock evaporated. The officer had genuinely believed, knowing the caliber of the staff over many years, such a catastrophe couldn't happen there. The fact is, such things can happen anywhere.

People become emotionally attached to their investments for one reason or another. That's another reason to consult with a third party who has no emotional involvement and can look strictly at the numbers. You may care very much about an investment, but it doesn't care about you. It simply is what it is. It doesn't have a heart. It doesn't have a soul. It simply functions according to the way it's designed to function.

Even if your grandfather implored you, from his deathbed, to never sell that stock, go ahead and do what you must. Your grandfather had no crystal ball for economic trends. However, such misplaced loyalty isn't what I mostly see. Rather, people take their own investment decisions too personally. They did the research, they made the purchase, and they told their friends; selling it would feel as if they were admitting a mistake.

What they don't take into account is that though the investment may have been perfectly appropriate the day they bought it, things have changed every day since. What might have been a really good investment for them at the time is not so good any longer.

During your working years, when you make an investment aimed at the future, you can just hang in there during a down year, as your broker might say, and all will be well. That's true as long as you aren't tapping that investment as an income source. Your paycheck takes care of your expenses. You don't need or want income from your investments, so you can reinvest the returns.

However, on the day you retire, your focus turns to living expenses and how you'll pay for them without wages. If your investments are all subject to market risk, a big loss will hurt you immediately and dramatically.

So, it's a matter of sheer mathematics – how the numbers fall. That's why I emphasize that the best way to avoid such a predicament is to allocate your money between income money and the money you're not going to need to spend for a while.

How do you figure out how much you'll need? Answering that question is why retirement counseling is so helpful in focusing clients' goals, dreams, and expectations. My clients and I look at their assets and income expectations (up to age one hundred) and see if we can make the numbers work with an acceptable level of risk.

Reasonable risks

We face many financial risks: the stock market, inflation, taxes, interest rates, erosion of purchasing power, and, of course, health. However, for most of us, the mention of financial risk conjures up, first and foremost, the stock market. If a retiree is heavily and unwisely invested in risky equities, one bad market is all it takes to derail his or her dreams. Bad markets are inevitable. What the market gives, it can quickly take away.

A market crash is defined as any time the market falls by at least 20 percent. Since 1929, the market has dropped by at least 20 percent seventeen times. On average, that's a crash about every five years. Economists say that, on average, it takes six point six years to recover from a crash – and you can see the irony there. Yes, those are averages: Some recoveries take longer, some come swiftly. But if you're wondering why you don't seem to be making money in the market, statistics like that can be illuminating.

If you look at a hundred-year chart of the stock market, you can see common eighteen-year cycles in the Dow Jones average. For example, from 1946 to 1964 the market had a nice rally, hitting 1,000 for the first time. Then, for the next eighteen years, from 1964 to 1982, it chopped. People were frustrated with the market. Then, from 1982 to 2000, we saw the biggest eighteen-year segment in history – before the bear came back to visit.

Even within the eighteen-year bear market cycle, historically we have seen several sucker rallies, as from 2003 to 2007, when people think the good old times are back, but then down we go again.

It's not that you should keep away from the stock market – not at all. Most of my clients have exposure to the stock market. It's not the stock market that's bad. What's bad is how you use it. The market can be your friend or it can be your foe.

An old rule of thumb for determining risk was that you should subtract your age from one hundred; the result is the maximum percentage you should have at risk. If you're eighty years old, for example, you should have no more than 20 percent of your money at risk, with 80 percent in non-risk assets. This rule of thumb can give people a common-sense perspective on investment, but only a general one. Your specific needs can make all the difference.

A knowledgeable and experienced financial planner has seen countless situations like yours and has perspective on what will work and what will not. Each type of investment – including bonds as well as stocks – has a type of risk associated with it.

What investors typically hear is that they need to keep their portfolios heavy in stocks and light on bonds during accumulation years, and then shift toward the opposite as they approach retirement. That does sound like the old rule of thumb that I just mentioned, but it's not as simple as that.

Assessing market risk is far more complicated than determining a simple bond/stock balance. Bonds have long been portrayed as safer than equities, but they carry a considerable risk right now that few people seem to understand. Talking heads on television suggest putting money in bonds, saying that out of the last thirty years, bonds have only lost money in, perhaps, one.

And that's true. But what these talking heads fail to mention is that there is a direct relationship between bond prices and interest rates. As interest rates drop, the value of a bond increases. Think back to about 1980, when the prime rate peaked at about 21 percent; as the rate fell in the ensuing years, bonds got quite a boost. Now, interest rates are down toward zero. They cannot drop much more. Which way do you think they'll go? As rates rise, your bonds will lose principal. You might have a mutual fund with 100 percent U.S. government securities – and you'll lose principal if those rates go up. That's what would happen, guaranteed.

For example, let's say the ten-year Treasury yield is at 3 percent. If that were to rise just one percentage point, to 4 percent, you'd have a 33 percent hit on the principal of the bond funds, losing a third. The last time we had a double-digit principal hit was in 1994. In 1994 the ten-year went from 6.5 to 8 percent. On average, people lost 20 percent of their principal in their U.S. government guaranteed funds, municipal bond funds, high-yield funds, or corporate bond funds – any of those bond funds.

That was 1994. It's been that long. When interest rates go up, bond funds get nailed. I'm sure you've seen those asset allocation pie charts. They show your stocks: large cap, mid-, and small; growth and value; international and emerging markets. They also show bond components. The allocation is all presented as, say, 60/40: 60 percent at risk and 40 percent in bonds. As you get older, you're supposed to increase your exposure to bonds, or your "safe money."

However, now that interest rates are this low, that safe money is not safe at all. The interest rate risk is very real. So is principal risk if you're invested in, say, municipal bonds that have been increasingly subject to default in a struggling economy. It's important to make sure your portfolio takes into consideration those two bond risks, in addition to the risks of stocks.

One-size-fits-all financial advice can hurt people who blindly heed it. Your portfolio deserves better than that. It should be developed with the sophistication that reflects investment realities and fundamental rules. Investors do get way out of whack with what's reasonable. Recently, I talked to a man in his early eighties who is 100 percent at risk and can't understand why he's not deriving enough income.

Your portfolio should also account for inflation, which poses another major risk to your wealth. Inflation is a silent killer. In a quarter century, the cost of things has doubled. In order to maintain his or her lifestyle, a retiree whose income is $60,000 a year today likely will need an income of $120,000 thirty years from now.

The likelihood of being able to increase that income on your own is very small. In most cases, you'll find yourself spending the assets you would need to generate that additional income. So, you won't have double the income. You'll have less.

For example, think about how much money you were making in 1986. In the ensuing years, your increasing paycheck kept inflation at bay. As long as you kept getting those raises, you were all right. Now, in retirement, you probably have two sources of income: Social Security and your own assets. Very few people have a pension any more, and I believe you can forget about expecting Social Security benefits to increase.

So, that leaves you with your nest egg funds, and whatever you saved during those working years. If you draw on those assets to the maximum, you'll simply have to do without when the price of a loaf of bread triples. People don't realize that soon enough. They get the feeling things are becoming more expensive, but they don't calculate how they will fare if they continue down that road of spending.

I see people having to get reverse mortgages just so they can remain in their homes. That's only a temporary fix, and they can only get up to half the value of those assets. Even if they can stay in their houses, they may struggle to pay the heating and electric bills. If they live too long, the reverse mortgage alone won't be enough.

You can avoid that predicament with some forethought and insight into the markets and how they work. The ultimate goal is to see your assets rise, year by year, even growing in years when the market falls. The first item in your retirement rulebook should be that everything you always believed about investing is no longer true. Now, your emphasis must be on income, so you don't run out of money before you die and instead can live happily ever after, however you define that.

While that's far from a guarantee, careful planning raises your prospects considerably and helps to assure that you have the money you need. A long and happy retirement can be yours, with many happy returns.

CHAPTER TWO

"What, Me Worry?"

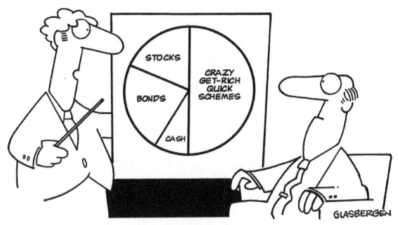

"I'd like you to consider a bold new strategy..."

Remember when you were a kid out on the schoolyard and the game wasn't going right? "Do-over! Do-over!" you would shout. It was that simple. You could stop the game and start over.

Once you're retired, there are no do-overs. You can't go back, erase the slate, and start over financially. Once the retirement party is over, you're done. Whatever you have is what has to last for the rest of your life.

During all your working years, you were saving for your future – for the retirement you envisioned, for travel, for medical needs, for however you anticipated using that money one day. Your goal was to leave it alone to grow. If it didn't, or if you had a loss, your financial adviser likely told you, "Hang in there, it'll come back." And, in time, it did. That's the way the game was played during those working years. However, when you retire, the game changes, and nobody gives you a new rulebook.

This is a different world. In many places, home values have dropped 30, 60, and even 70 percent. In the past, people thought they were going to be able to sell or refinance their homes for additional income. They used to think of a house as if it were an ATM. However, they can't count on that now, nor can they count on the volatile stock market. CD rates are at their lowest ever. The national debt was well over $15 trillion in early 2012 and is continuing to climb with no end in sight. Domestic production is in the tank. We import everything.

Those are sobering considerations, which add to the struggle to make ends meet. With retirees living longer than ever and inflation poised to jump to double digits again, we are inside a perfect storm. Everything seems to be lining up against retirees right now.

Perhaps the retirees' biggest obstacle is their own resistance to change. Many retirees have spent a lifetime building their assets and nurturing their nest eggs. Now, it's time to protect those funds. What you need to do now is find the best way to convert all your hard work into an income – for life.

A retiree's biggest mistake

Consider this scenario: At age forty, two gentlemen each invest $100,000 in the market and they both get returns over the course of the next twenty-five years. In fact, they get exactly the same returns – but in the opposite order. One has good years while the other has bad years, and vice versa, but, ultimately, after twenty-five years, their returns come out the same: Each has averaged 8.98 percent and each now has an account that has grown to $630,294.

Then, they both retire at age sixty-five. Each starts withdrawing $40,000 a year from their accounts, and each continues to invest that money the same way. Over the next fifteen years, once again they get the exact same returns, but, once again, in the opposite order. At age seventy-nine, one of them is broke and the other has $1.2 million.

What has happened? The one who ended up broke had losses in the early years of his retirement, in the first three years. The one who ended up wealthy didn't have those losses until the last three years.

The lesson here should be clear: What worked well for both of them during their accumulation years became a disaster for one of them during their retirement years.

Whether their losses came early or late didn't matter when neither was withdrawing money. Yet, after they retired and were tapping their accounts, one found it impossible to recover from an early hit.

If you're drawing income from a fluctuating account in retirement, you're shooting yourself – not in the foot, but in the head. I call this financial Russian roulette. You don't know which year the market's going to go down, but it will go down, and when it does, it can do you in for good.

So, never put that gun to your head. Never draw income from a fluctuating account, whether it's a mutual fund, an equity account, or anything that rises and falls with the markets.

You might hear something like this at a cocktail party: "I'm so brilliant!" someone will brag, after riding the wave of a bullish year. "I had $100,000, I took out $20,000 last year, and my account is *still worth* $100,000. I'm brilliant!"

Yet, will that person be bragging if, stars in his eyes, he grabs another $20,000 next year, only to see the market tumble 20 percent instead of rising that much? The remaining $80,000 will not only fail to grow, it will slump deeply. After withdrawing 20 percent, the market could slam him with 20 percent more, and there's an accelerating effect to losses when you withdraw funds from a falling account. He would never recover from that. It only takes one down year to wreak such havoc.

I can't imagine hearing these words at a cocktail party: "I'm so brilliant! I had $100,000, I took out $20,000, and, gosh, I think I've got more than $50,000 left in my account!"

When you're not withdrawing money, this isn't an issue. Down years come along regularly, as do up years, and eventually you ride to a gain. However, once you start using an account for income, you lose time's power of healing and growth. While this is a huge consideration, it seems few people understand it until they've been retired for a number of years and realize what they've been doing just doesn't work any longer. Many find it hard to believe until I show them the chart below.

Distribution Phase ($630,294 Beginning Balance)

	Investor A				Investor B	
Age	*Portfolio Year End Value	Annual Return	Withdrawals		Annual Returns	*Portfolio Year End Value
65	$630,294					$ 630,294
66	$439,906	-23.86%	($40,000)		27.61%	$672,034
67	$347,293	-11.96%	($40,000)		19.04%	$713,314
68	$233,632	-21.21%	($40,000)		31.82%	$755,584
69	$248,886	23.65%	($40,000)		7.14%	$796,123
70	$238,354	11.84%	($40,000)		16.11%	$837,406
71	$218,233	8.34%	($40,000)		9.57%	$878,207
72	$221,182	19.68%	($40,000)		-4.02%	$917,854
73	$189,675	3.84%	($40,000)		5.68%	$958,375
74	$168,529	9.94%	($40,000)		12.91%	$999,613
75	$117,726	-6.41%	($40,000)		17.66%	$1,041,378
76	$100,376	19.24%	($40,000)		26.72%	$1,084,161
77	$64,853	4.46%	($40,000)		-3.74%	$1,123,755
78	$32,292	11.47%	($40,000)		11.47%	$1,165,044
79	-	-3.74%	($40,000)		4.46%	$1,205,564
80	-	26.72%	($40,000)		19.24%	$1,247,883
81	-	17.66%	($40,000)		-6.41%	$1,287,083
82	-	12.91%	($40,000)		9.94%	$1,328,363
83	-	5.68%	($40,000)		3.84%	$1,368,873
84	-	-4.02%	($40,000)		19.68%	$1,411,567
85	-	9.57%	($40,000)		8.34%	$1,452,744
86	-	16.11%	($40,000)		11.84%	$1,494,464
87	-	7.14%	($40,000)		23.65%	$1,537,998
88	-	31.82%	($40,000)		-21.21%	$1,574,736
89	-	19.04%	($40,000)		-11.96%	$1,612,853
90	-	27.61%	($40,000)		-23.86%	$1,649,005
		8.98%			8.98%	

* The annual returns experienced by Investor A are in the exact opposite order of those experienced by Investor B. Investing exposes your assets to risk and accounts can lose value. Figures shown are used only to illustrate concepts. When investing, actual returns may be more or less than illustrated.

Accumulation Phase ($100,000 Initial Investment)

Age	*Portfolio Year End Value	Investor A Annual Return	Withdrawals	Investor B Annual Returns	*Portfolio Year End Value
40	$ 100,000				
41	$76,140	-23.86%		27.61%	$127,610
42	$67,034	-11.96%		19.04%	$151,907
43	$52,816	-21.21%		31.82%	$200,244
44	$65,307	23.65%		7.14%	$214,541
45	$73,039	11.84%		16.11%	$249,104
46	$79,131	8.34%		9.57%	$272,943
47	$94,703	19.68%		-4.02%	$261,971
48	$98,340	3.84%		5.68%	$276,851
49	$108,115	9.94%		12.91%	$312,592
50	$101,185	-6.41%		17.66%	$367,796
51	$120,653	19.24%		26.72%	$466,071
52	$126,034	4.46%		-3.74%	$448,640
53	$140,490	11.47%		11.47%	$500,099
54	$135,236	-3.74%		4.46%	$522,403
55	$171,371	26.72%		19.24%	$622,913
56	$201,635	17.66%		-6.41%	$582,985
57	$227,666	12.91%		9.94%	$640,933
58	$240,597	5.68%		3.84%	$665,545
59	$230,925	-4.02%		19.68%	$796,524
60	$253,025	9.57%		8.34%	$862,955
61	$293,787	16.11%		11.84%	$965,128
62	$314,763	7.14%		23.65%	$1,193,381
63	$414,921	31.82%		-21.21%	$940,265
64	$493,922	19.04%		-11.96%	$827,809
65	$630,294	27.61%		-23.86%	$630,294
		8.98%		8.98%	

* The annual returns experienced by Investor A are in the exact opposite order of those experienced by Investor B. Investing exposes your assets to risk and accounts can lose value. Figures shown are used only to illustrate concepts. When investing, actual returns may be more or less than illustrated.

If you're pulling income out of a fluctuating account, you will get crushed. If you're doing so, stop now, or I guarantee – and I don't use that word lightly – that you will not have the income you will need and want for the rest of your life. After 2008, so many people came into my office, trying to understand why that $2 million or $4 million that was supposed to see them through their remaining years was gone. They never imagined they'd be thinking about a job at McDonald's.

"The new Tax Reform plan is simple and efficient.
Toss all of your money into the air, whatever
lands in your pocket, you get to keep."

Don't count on Social Security

As we've seen, withdrawing money while it is vulnerable to the markets can compound your losses – and that compounds your problems in retirement, particularly because people are living longer than ever.

When Social Security was enacted in 1935, benefits started at age sixty-five and the average life expectancy was only sixty-three. Today, a man's life expectancy is eighty-five; a woman's is eighty-eight. That's only the average; some people will live to well over one hundred. It's hard, both for individuals and the government, to plan for that many years of retirement. According to a recent analysis, unless there's legislative action, the Social Security Administration will be broke by 2036. In addition, at that point most baby boomer retirees will still be going strong.

Most likely, the system will change. It could become subject to means testing, which means you would only get a Social Security benefit if it was determined that you needed it. If you had the means to do without it, you wouldn't get it. If you have money, the reasoning for means testing goes, you can fund your own retirement. That would be quite a dis-incentive, then, to do well in your financial life. If you spent more than you earned, gambled and drank your pay away, or bought things you couldn't afford, the government would reward you with Social Security benefits. In contrast, if you were wise and frugal, and gave up some luxuries so you'd have the means to get by in retirement, the government would say, "Well, fine. You have enough money. You don't need Social Security." Never mind that you put money into the system for all those years – in fact, you probably contributed more than those who would later find themselves without the means and would qualify for Social Security.

You may have noticed that Social Security benefits aren't rising the way prices are. The government recently eliminated food and energy from the inflation calculation for Social Security – and if you're retired, what else are you spending money on besides food and energy?

The tax issues of Social Security are another catch. When the Social Security program was established, the government promised that you wouldn't be taxed on this money again. Today, as much as 85 percent of your Social Security benefit becomes taxable every year – you paid the tax, and now you pay a tax again. The early promises apparently meant nothing.

A stool with broken legs

Still, when working with retirees, I count Social Security as a potential retirement benefit. I basically assume there will be no inflation increases on Social Security, and that at some point the government is just going to treat it like a regular pension. If you think about it, most pensions in the world do not have annual increases.

Once upon a time, you could depend on the pension you got from that factory job that you held so long. For years and years, retirement counselors talked about "the three-legged stool." You would have three legs to cover your retirement. The first would be Social Security, the second would be your own assets, and the third would be the company pension for your loyal years of service.

Few companies today offer pensions. Retirees who had been promised pensions had them taken away. We've had situations where portions of a retirement account were sold when the company was sold – and employees lost what they had thought was a company match that was theirs to keep. Retirees no longer can expect to work at a company for twenty or thirty years and get a gold watch and lifelong pension.

That means the three-legged stool is down to two. As the Social Security rules change, you can't count on that leg anymore. You're basically left with just whatever you've done or can do for yourself.

A three-legged stool is reasonably stable, but if you take away any of those legs it topples right over. That's what we're seeing right now. So many retirees are going back to work. They've had their stool topple on them, and so they're looking for other things to do. It has gotten to the point where every individual, young or old, has to step up and take responsibility for their retirement – or it isn't going to happen.

Health insurance issues

That responsibility includes making sure you're covered for health care – a scary prospect because costs have been out of control. We all see the underpinnings of why health expenses and insurance costs are going up so precipitously. I have a client who has been a surgeon about twenty years. "I've been doing this long enough that I pretty much know when I sit down with somebody and we do a little bit of blood work and talk about their symptoms, I feel certain what the issue is. I know what's going on." But, he said, "I can't just tell them what it is right there. There's that one percent chance that I'm incorrect, so I have to order $50,000 worth of tests just to make sure – because if I'm wrong and I get sued, I lose everything." He thinks that he single-handedly could save as much as $1 million a year in unnecessary tests; without tort reform, he believes, he cannot do his job effectively.

And as costs rise, retirees face a future of fewer government benefits. Medicare and Medicaid benefits are so seriously underfunded right now that benefits are being cut. More and more doctors today simply refuse to accept any Medicare patients. The federal government mandates that if they take one they have to take them all, and they only get whatever compensation the federal government says they should get. If it costs a physician $20 to do a procedure and the federal government only reimburses $8, it's impossible to make that up on volume. As a result, it has become more and more difficult for retirees to find doctors they can see. They're starting to feel like the Canadians who would come to the United States and pay cash for services because at home they were on such a long waiting list.

I know a pediatrician who at least doesn't have to deal with Medicare cases – but he doesn't even take insurance anymore. Patients pay him a retainer for access to him and basically pay for services. He eliminated insurance.

So among the swirl of concerns that retirees have as they're trying to sort out how to properly prepare for the many years ahead, they must face the fact that they indeed *have* many years ahead – and health issues will be unavoidable.

"If it costs $1300 a day to be in the hospital, how much
is a 15% tip for the person who brings my meals?"

Cost of long-term care

I recently got a call from a client's daughter. "I'm here at the hospital with my dad and mom," she said. "Dad had a stroke, and Mom is absolutely beside herself. She's afraid he's going to die, and she's afraid he's going to live."

"What do you mean?" I asked.

"Well, she doesn't want him to die, of course, but she's afraid if he lives she won't have the money that she needs to take care of him. She can't lift him. She doesn't know that she's going to be able to make that work. And she's sad."

"Listen, they're going to be fine," I was able to tell the daughter. "They've got all of their long-term-care planning in place. We hope your dad lives, and if he does, your mom is going to be fine. If he happens to pass away, your mom is still going to be fine."

He survived. I was glad to be able to reassure that family – but that's not always the case. Unless the foundation is in place for dealing with such expenses, they can be devastating.

In my mind, the single biggest risk that a retiree has isn't health costs but long-term health costs. Long-term-care insurance has been a bait-and-switch, as Social Security was. People have paid for such plans – in some cases for ten or twenty years – just to see their premium go up so much when they were closer to needing the benefit that they had to drop their coverage. Some insurers have stopped selling long-term-care coverage altogether, as people live longer and use more benefits.

The baby boomers' optimism has actually hurt them when it comes to health issues. They don't seem to believe they're going to get sick or die. Once, at a seminar, when I asked, "What's the chance of dying?" one man responded, "Fifty percent." I said, "Man, I need to find out what your plan is." I suppose he thought I meant the chances of needing long-term care. Or maybe he's even more optimistic than his fellow boomers.

You can be sure your chance of dying is one hundred percent. And before we die we're going to get sick. Things that worked for us our whole lives all of a sudden aren't going to work anymore – and that's true not only for investment styles but also for body parts.

A day in a long-term-care facility averages over $200, or about $6,000 a month, so it adds up quickly. Oxygen or other needs greatly increase the expenses. I had a client who was paying $8,500 a month for long-term care. The cost of coverage is hefty. The risk of no coverage can be catastrophic.

When I ask people why they don't have long-term-care insurance, they consistently mention two reasons: Number one, they tell me it's too expensive. "It could cost me several thousand a year, and that's a lot of money," they say. Or: "I guess I could afford it, except that if I don't go to a long-term-care facility I lose all that money," meaning the insurer wins if death comes suddenly from a heart attack, say, or getting hit by a bus.

Baby boomers, however, are such a political power that their sheer numbers change things. The 1980s were their play day – they were coming into money and opportunities, and it was a decade of excess. And now, as a lot of boomers are facing the need for long-term care, insurance companies are changing their products.

Asset-based long-term-care protection allows you to put money into a plan but get it back if you don't need long-term care. Imagine you were to set money aside in an account that's 100 percent liquid. You could take it back any time. You get a few percent in interest. If you go into long-term care, you can get up to four times the amount you put in to cover that need. If you die without needing long-term care, the account will pay as much as twice what you put into this plan to your beneficiaries. Such a plan exists.

Or you can buy life insurance policies from some companies with a rider that covers long-term care if you need it. In other words, you can get your death benefit while you're still alive; otherwise, it's regular life insurance, paid to your beneficiary. I think that's going to be the wave of the future. I expect that traditional long-term-care insurance likely will disappear soon just because of that change. That is one way that retirees can be reassured that long-term-care insurance is still an affordable, worthwhile benefit to protect their assets.

And it's a critical protection. The need for long-term care is the single biggest financial risk that retirees have. Everybody has fire insurance, but only five out of 1,000 people will actually have a house burn down in their lifetime. But when it comes to long-term-care insurance,

700 out of 1,000 people will spend at least ninety days in a long-term-care facility, but only six percent of people over the age of 65 have any kind of protection at all. They may be saving on premiums, but the best of financial plans goes awry if suddenly the retiree needs an additional $10,000 a month for long-term care.

Without long-term care, and without sufficient medical coverage, you can be wiped out. I recently heard of an older couple who had been married for many decades, and they were divorcing – not because they didn't love each other anymore, but because he was in a long-term-care facility and they were trying to protect some of the money for her.

The lesson: If you don't plan sufficiently, you might be tempted to take such drastic steps to avoid being wiped out financially. But if you take action, you can have peace of mind knowing that you and your assets will be all right. No matter what happens to your health, you can still have something to leave to future generations.

© Randy Glasbergen
www.glasbergen.com

"Allowing for inflation and the rising cost of tuition, you'll
need to save 40 billion dollars for your children's education."

Erosion of spending power

Imagine a million-dollar bill lying on the table in front of you. Think of it as representing every asset you have – your house, your retirement accounts, your savings account, your checking account. But beyond that, think of it as also including everything that you did without. Those vacations you didn't take. The cars you didn't buy. It's everything that you did over the course of your lifetime to accumulate a nest egg. That's what the million-dollar bill represents.

"That's great," you may be thinking. "I can make that work well. I can live on that for the rest of my life."

But then some things happen. One is inflation. Inflation takes away your purchasing power, so there goes part of your million. But that's not the only thing. Medicare costs are going up, even as coverage is going down – and your need for health services is bound to increase. The biggest drain is this: You have to pay taxes. Taxes on your retirement accounts, taxes on your current income.

That still leaves a nice chunk of change. But you could have more. You have the power to keep a bigger portion of that million.

Will you keep up with inflation? We're in for some serious inflation, due to the way the government has run up deficits and tried to spend its way out of recession. Consider how much you paid for your first house. Was it $10,000? How much did you pay for your last house? Perhaps $400,000? It's nicer, I'm sure, but is it forty times nicer? Inflation raised the price.

Meanwhile, what was happening to your pay? What were you earning in, say, 1986, and recently as you drew your last few paychecks before retirement? Perhaps your pay rose from $40,000 to $100,000 during those years – that's a typical range that I see. Your paycheck adjusted for inflation. But once you get to retirement, those inflation increases stop.

You may remember the days of the WIN buttons, "Whip Inflation Now," during the Gerald Ford administration, when we were facing the ravages of double-digit inflation. In those days, retirees could get a high rate on Certificates of Deposit, far more than today's minuscule rates, and many expected that would get them through.

Then, as now, they were actually going backward. Taxes, too, are increasingly eroding your spending power. There has never been a time when CD rates minus taxes have beaten inflation. CD rates are a trailing indicator of inflation. Investors were getting 12 or 14 percent, but inflation was 10 to 12 percent. After taxes, they were losing money. It's the same today, though the rates are so low that they hardly create a tax issue.

But even the little you do still earn on a CD is taxed, and what's more, it counts against your Social Security threshold, so you are taxed on part of your benefit as well. It's a similar story with tax-free municipal bonds. People are impressed that they don't pay income tax on the earnings – yet, for retirees, those earnings do count toward the calculation for the tax on your Social Security. "Tax-free" is relative.

Today's prices are going up, regardless of what you might hear. Inflation is bound to rise, and it's going to leave retirees in the dust. There's no way they can keep up. They will be needing to use more and more of their nest egg just to pay for food. I do believe interest rates are going to go up, but they'll trail inflation. The rates won't keep up. Neither will retirees.

You can take action to protect yourself and prevent the erosion of your spending power – if you wake up in time. Being retired ten years often is what it takes to wake up a retiree. Even so, only one retiree in twenty will have the income he or she needs and wants throughout retirement. That's a very sad statistic. The main reason for the shortfall is lack of planning.

"I'm going to be that one in twenty," a gentleman once told me.

"Why is that?" I inquired.

"Well, when I retire I'm going to have a plan on how I am going to spend my money."

I congratulated him but reminded him that all twenty of those retirees also believe they have a plan. Things happen to knock you off course. Are you protected from the whims of the stock market? Will taxes lay you low? Will you have a reasonable portion of health and be able to cover your medical costs? Will you be able to beat inflation? Will you, in short, be able to pay the bills for the rest of your life?

Retirement plan surprises

Retirement plans in particular are a major source of tax surprises that erode the value of assets you thought you had for your golden years. Countless people sock their money away into 401(k)s and IRAs for retirement, deferring their income tax on those investments until they withdraw the money. Retirees might be able to push off the tax issues for many years, but eventually they must be faced.

Those tax issues are difficult to deal with – but if it weren't for such accounts, most people would have no retirement savings. Retirement accounts at least give them some assets. When retirees balk at paying the deferred tax on those accounts, I respond: "Well, you've got a problem. The tax has to be paid, or you can't spend the money."

In essence, a retirement plan comes with a mortgage. You might see $1 million in your account, but in reality you don't have that. You have more like $650,000, and the IRS has a $350,000 claim. You can get your $650,000, but how can you reduce the IRS's take?

When these plans were introduced, I thought that finally the federal government was doing something that helps the little guy. But after years of working with retirees, it's clear to me that the government is doing what's best for itself.

Most people don't withdraw from a retirement account until six months after they turn seventy. That's because that's the age when they are required to do so. And then they only take out the minimum required. People are retiring and yet they aren't pulling much of their retirement savings from their plans. They keep postponing those taxes as long as possible.

Nonetheless, if they live 25 years taking out just the minimum on, say, a $500,000 account, depending on returns, they easily could end up paying nearly $500,000 in taxes on those distributions. From a tax perspective, it would be tempting to liquidate the account at age 65, because the tax bite even in the 40 percent bracket would only be about 200,000, a bargain by comparison. I'm not saying that's the right thing to do, but it would at least give less to Uncle Sam.

And what happens when the retiree eventually dies? Unless the account is left to a spouse, everything that remains in it is going to be taxed in a very high bracket because the money is paid out in one calendar year immediately. It's fully taxable as a lump sum, unless the heir takes it as a stretch IRA, receiving only minimal annual payouts. Never has a beneficiary come to me and said, "Okay, Mom and Dad wanted me to stretch it, so I'll stretch it." It's more like, "I'm inheriting 100 grand! So, sure, I have to lose $30,000 or $40,000 in taxes, but, hey, that's 60 grand I didn't have yesterday."

When it comes to retirement accounts, if we can do some tax planning and save somebody an additional $25,000 or $30,000, we consider that a win. That's money they wouldn't otherwise have seen.

Roth IRA and other conversions

Let me give you an example, a gentleman has several million dollars in an IRA that he probably won't spend during his lifetime. That money was going to be annihilated by estate taxes and income taxes.

With about $1.5 million dollars of property that he had acquired over the previous 40 years, and a cost basis of only about $250,000. He wanted to make a gift when he died to a local university, so he could donate the $1.5 million in property. The university could then buy a life insurance policy on the gentleman for $2 million.

In other words, he was able to pull $1.5 million out of his estate as a charitable donation, and in return he got a $2 million value to pass on to his heirs without a tax hit. He also was able to convert $1 million in his traditional IRA into a Roth IRA so that its earnings would not be taxable upon withdrawal.

The net benefit in his situation would be several hundred thousand dollars of taxes that would not have to be paid. It could be done by taking advantage of rules that exist today. And one of those rules is the conversion to a Roth IRA, established in 1997 under the Taxpayer Relief Act and named for its sponsor, Sen. William Roth of Delaware.

Much has been written on whether it's wise to convert a traditional retirement account into a Roth IRA. There are situations where a Roth is appropriate and others in which it's not.

The advantage of the Roth is that all of the money that you pull out of a Roth and all of the growth that you get from it for your entire life is tax-free – and not only for your life but also for as long as your children and grandchildren live. The disadvantage is that you have a $6,000 per year limit on how much you can put in and you can only add if you have earned income.

You can convert money from a traditional IRA to a Roth, but every dollar that you convert to a Roth becomes taxable immediately. So even though it's tax-free forever, it does create a tax consequence when you're taking that money out of the traditional IRA (unless you earned it in federal service, in which case earnings can be moved to an Roth and be tax-exempt forever, a provision that's clearly the work of a Capitol Hill politician).

The "live-on, leave-on" concept that we discussed earlier is a good rule of thumb for deciding whether to convert to a Roth IRA. The live-on money, again, is the money you'll spend during your retirement; the leave-on money is what you probably won't spend in your lifetime and will leave to the kids and grandkids. If it's leave-on money, it makes sense to convert that to a Roth. With live-on money, it really depends. My rule of thumb is that if you're not going to spend the money for at least ten years, it probably makes sense to convert it to a Roth. But if you're going to spend that money in the next ten years, then it probably doesn't make sense to incur that additional tax because the money will be gone before it can grow enough to make the expense worthwhile.

Suppose you have $100,000 and you convert that to a Roth. You pay $30,000 in taxes to do so, which leaves you

$70,000. Depending upon how long you live, that may grow back to $100,000 or even $150,000. It's exciting that you can give the kids $150,000 tax-free.

However, consider a concept that I call a super-Roth. With a super-Roth, you take that same $100,000 in the IRA and do a conversion that creates a $300,000 tax-free benefit to your beneficiaries – double the Roth benefit that you might have expected – and it's *still* tax-free.

How could that be? Let's say, for example, that you know you are never going to spend that $100,000. It's money you will leave to your heirs. So you start drawing from that IRA, perhaps $10,000 a year. You use that $10,000 to buy life insurance and also to cover the deferred taxes. Let's say the life insurance you purchase has a $300,000 benefit upon your death, and your heirs get that money tax-free. What you are doing is slowly using your IRA withdrawals to pay the premium on life insurance – and by so doing, you have tripled the benefit for the beneficiaries. If your intent from the start was to pass on that money, why not provide those heirs with three times the original amount in the account? If you convert it to a Roth, it might in time only double.

Setting up a stretch IRA

Many retirees are concerned, however, about how their heirs will use that money left to them. Even if they don't get the money tax-free, they may be more than willing to grab whatever they can in a lump sum and spend it on a Porsche. You may know your children wouldn't do that, but some parents aren't quite so confident. There are steps they can take, however, to protect their nest egg's fate.

I have helped many clients over the years set up stretch IRAs, as I mentioned earlier, in which the money can be distributed not as a lump sum but as a continued monthly payment. On a $400,000 account, an heir may be able to take from that, say, $1,500 a month every month for the rest of his or her life.

"Here's the deal," we tell the heir. "Your dad [or your grandfather] would like you to take this as income, $1,500 a month for as long as you live. Or, well, if you really want, you can take it as $225,000 in cash today." I have never had anybody take the monthly income. None of them seem to care that they'll be paying $175,000 in taxes. They go for the big dough, and with IRAs there is typically nothing you can do.

However, if you set up the super-Roth that I just described, you can have that pay into a trust that would prevent the heirs from taking out anything other than what you specified. You gain control over what your heirs do with the money, because you might not know which of your heirs will do the right thing. Some of them will be very good with money. Some of them may be naïve or irresponsible.

Getting the right advice

Many retirees feel overwhelmed by the weight of their concerns, but rest assured: Your worries are normal and shared by countless others. Everybody has similar concerns, and often they don't know whom to talk to about them.

Most people don't realize that the financial world is stacked against them. Much of the advice you're offered throughout your life has had only a little to do with what you need and a lot to do with what the adviser is selling. Stockbrokers and insurance agents have a product to sell and don't have a fiduciary responsibility. If you sit down with a car salesman, you have your defenses up. You know he gets his pay for persuading you to buy. But for some reason when people sit down with a stockbroker or other adviser, they assume that person has their best interest in mind. They seem not to realize they're being sold a product.

And those products are likely to engender too much risk for a retirement portfolio. Different things are riskier in retirement than prior to retirement. The exact same asset that once served you well may now be inappropriate for this stage of life. Yet it's hard to switch from accumulation to distribution. It's not as easy as flicking a switch. You still may be thinking, "I'm going to need money, so I have to step out and take that risk. I have to get that growth."

That's not likely what you'll get. Although you still may need growth, you can't have all your assets in growth or there's no chance that money will last. You cannot take the risks you once did. During your working years, if you lost a job, you found another. If you suffered a loss in the market, you left those assets alone and watched them recover in time. If you had health problems, you could count on your employer's insurance.

But all of those things are different once you retire. If you have bad health after you retire, you can be out of money. If you take a loss in the market, or simply don't get a good enough return, you can be out of money. Inflation kicks in, you're out of money. The pitfalls from which you could recover prior to retirement can swat you down for good during retirement. You stand at a crossroads, and you need impartial, practical, and wise advice.

Retirees' biggest worries

If retirees' biggest concern is having enough income for life, then the second biggest concern is protecting that income from taxes – and making sure their assets go to their heirs, not the taxman, upon death.

Retirees by and large have a generous spirit but they want to retain control over how their money is distributed.

They don't necessarily believe the government will put it to the best use. Estate planning is therefore a big concern among retirees: how to pass the money on in a tax-efficient way, in a manner that is going to reserve the money for how you want it to be spent.

The retiree has so many other questions to juggle. Will I be able to afford health care or the cost of extended care? Will I be able to keep ahead of inflation? Will I have liquid funds available in case of an emergency? Will I be able to contribute to charity, and how can I make sure the money goes to those in need and not to the IRS or lawyers?

Yes, there are many worries and considerations that could keep you awake at night. It can be reassuring to know that so many others are in your shoes, with the same concerns – and that's been the case for generations. These are common issues as we get older, and the key is to take action. When you set your priorities, you're going to be far better able to chart your retirement.

Retiring on Your Terms

"I finally put something aside for my retirment.
I put aside my plans to retire."

My father spent most all his life on the small farm where I grew up – in fact, having to milk cows every morning and night was my motivation to go to college. My father also had a job in the city, so he was up at three in the morning and working until sundown every day. He finally retired and sold the property and moved into the city. I was a little concerned about him because he had been going eighteen hours a day every day for forty years.

"Dad," I said when I called him one day about six months later, "are you doing all right? How has retirement been going for you?"

"Well, Jim," he said, "I wake up in the morning with nothing to do, and I go to bed with it half done."

As retirees contemplate the years ahead, they have a preconceived vision of what it will be like. They embrace an image of how they'll live, what they'll do – and it often really doesn't reflect what they'll truly be trying to accomplish. "I'm retired now," they may be thinking. "I'm done. I'm not doing anything anymore." But almost nobody is done. Everybody ends up doing something.

With years of good health and energy ahead, these will be some of the most robust years of life, with expanding horizons and much to do and see. However, it's most certainly a new phase with new perspectives. People entering retirement aren't always ready for that. It sneaks up on them.

From go-go to no-go

There are three phases of retirement. They have been called the *go-go,* the *slow-go*, and the *no-go*.

The *go-go* phase comes during the first several years of retirement, when people want to travel and do all the things that they didn't do while they were working. They have the health, money and energy to begin tackling a list of life goals – the safari in Africa, the visit to the old country, the sojourn in Australia. That's typically the mindset during the first five to ten years of retirement.

After about a decade, retirees go into that *slow-go* mode where they still want to travel – but their health isn't quite as good, so they don't want to go as far. Trips are less exotic and less often. They're spending more time at home, and they're actually looking for things to do.

In about their late seventies, or early eighties, they hit the *no-go* phase, where they've been everywhere they want to go and seen what they want to see. In poorer health, they just can't do some things anymore. Their needs and wants are fewer, and they feel satisfied. They're not spending as much discretionary money. Many of their expenses are now medical, and their assets are just sitting there. By the time they reach this stage, whatever they haven't spent is pretty much going to go on to the next generation.

No time for rocking chairs

Retirement doesn't mean you'll be sitting on the porch rocking, with a mint julep. That's seldom the scenario. Nor is retirement about traveling all the time. To do that, you'd need to double or triple the income you had before you retired. It doesn't happen. What does happen is that retirees, once they see that life isn't quite as they expected it would be, get bored. They want to do something.

I've noticed that when couples head into retirement, the husband, if he was a traditional breadwinner, often is inclined to take it easy at home for a while, while the wife wants to go out and get more involved in community work. It's as if they can't both be in the house at the same time. Still, both men and women eventually want to be out of the house.

What retirees come to see is that they now have more control over time. They have more opportunity to decide when to get up, how to schedule the day – and when to go to work.

Very few people whom I see retiring at a younger age actually stay retired. They need to feel that they are still contributing. They have derived so much of their identity from what they did in the workplace. A lot of times they'll volunteer within their professional organization or take on some kind of emeritus duties that will give them a sense of still contributing to their life's work. People do want a sense of purpose. They want a sense of making this a better world.

Emotional reasons are why many retirees return to work. It's not necessarily about the money. It's about the connection. It's about having something to do.

Not all those Wal-Mart greeters are there out of necessity. Some sincerely like being around people. Many of my retired clients work. One works at a nursery three days a week, not because she must but because she wants to be around the flowers and the greenery and the people. She enjoys the social interaction.

I've had several recent clients who were at the point of retirement and, after talking with me about what they would do next, went back to their employers and asked to be kept on the payroll for, say, 30 hours a month. Most all the employers agreed; they could keep a good employee rather than go to the time and expense of replacing him or her. I believe this will increasingly become a trend.

In retirement, it comes down to this: How will you spend your time? You need to plan for your dreams. Are you going to spend time with your children? Are you going to go on a lot of vacations, or do volunteer work for charities? Will you write a book, learn a language, or launch a new endeavor?

"Okay, what are you going to do now," I ask clients entering their retirement years.

"Well, I'm going to travel more," they typically respond.

"Well, if you're going to travel more," I say, "you need to increase your budget for those expenses."

For some reason, people have been told that when they retire that they can live on 75 percent of their pre-retirement income. That's just not so. I have never seen anybody who lived on less money right after they retired than before they retired. That's particularly true in the early years. Nobody wants to go into retirement and just sit around the house. That's not the goal of not working. You can only watch so much daytime television before you go nuts.

Retirees need and want something to do. Their vision of retirement isn't what it actually is. After several years, they see that. They come to understand it far better than I could ever explain it.

That vision of sitting on the porch swing, rocking the days away, no longer leads to a contented sigh. It leads to a desire to rise up and start walking.

Go climb a tree

We get our impressions about what retirement should be like, and what we should do, from television and movies and well-intentioned friends. But what's best for you?

"Go climb a tree," I tell my clients.

Remember when you were 12 years old and you would climb a tree and sit there by yourself for a while? The world seemed yours to conquer. If you could do anything with your life, you asked yourself, what would it be?

When I suggest that, clients often start talking about dreams deferred and places they wanted to see. They always wanted to do this, or do that, but they never did because they got this job, or that job. Maybe they worked at a job they hated for thirty or forty years, and now they see a chance to finally do the work they really wanted to do and expand their horizons beyond the workplace walls. It's sad, actually.

So I suggest they climb that childhood tree and figure out what they want to do. "If you're like most people," I say, "I suspect that one of your big hopes right now is to do some traveling."

Most all retirees have a place in mind that they want to see or something they want to do. And I encourage them to do that first. Go ahead and plan for that trip, I suggest, and while you're doing that, let's talk about what else you want to do. Sometimes what happens is that once they've fulfilled that dream, they no longer want to retire just yet. Time no longer seems quite so pressing.

Getting organized

To purse a fulfilling retirement, then, you must find direction in your life. And part of finding direction is being organized.

To help you navigate your financial affairs – and to spare your executors a nightmare someday – I help clients organize their important documents. We start with the question, "What happens to your assets when you die?"

Ask anybody who as an adult has had to deal with the death of a parent. That's an experience a great many retirees have been through, and you'll hear how they had to go back and clean out mom and dad's house, trying to get things organized and finding papers. I find that the best planners are people who have just been through that difficult experience. They don't want their own children to have to go through it.

I work with clients to set up what looks almost like a treasure chest for them. It could even be labeled "Last gift to the children." Inside is a variety of information: funeral plans, location of assets, whether there is a safety deposit box, just to name a few. The goal is to consolidate information in one place in the house so it can easily be accessed not only by the retiree but also by whomever he or she chooses to tell about it – such as the children, or principal advisers. They know where the box is and what's in it. It's available and organized whenever the client needs to consult it – and it certainly simplifies matters in the event of death.

Retirees often ask whether they should keep those documents in the house or elsewhere, such as in a safety deposit box. If you put it in a safety deposit box, make sure that it's set up correctly so that the necessary people can access it if you can't do so yourself. If you're concerned about fire or theft, you can purchase a fire resistant box, if you so desire, and you can conceal it discreetly – just make sure the files are clearly recognizable so that loved ones can find them.

The advantage to keeping your documents at home is that you have quick access. You'll often need to add, review, or discard documents. You don't want to review those documents to the point of obsession, however. Knowing that your nest egg has to last you for the rest of your life can lead to monitoring it so closely that you find yourself watching the markets constantly all day long. Some retirees let their attitude and mood be determined by that. That's not retirement.

I once had a client with an $8 million portfolio who had been retired for going on twenty years. He watched CNBC every day, worried about each investment. After we set up a retirement plan, he began to relax, and after a few years, when we met for the annual review, his wife told me: "Oh, thank you. I finally feel like we're retired now." Her husband had left one tough full-time job and proceeded to take on another that was even more grueling. Now they could relax.

Taking the reins

Stress isn't a word that many people would want to associate with retirement. Bringing in an expert can greatly reduce the stress you might feel as you try to grasp your financial picture.

Whenever my car starts making odd sounds or the brakes start to squeak, I don't rip into the machinery and try to figure out what's wrong. That's a job for a qualified mechanic. When a pipe springs a leak in my house, I don't start tearing down walls. I hire a plumber. As we deal with so many aspects of daily living, we use experts.

So now, in retirement, as people face critical financial decisions, some want to try to figure it all out themselves. Decades of hard work behind them, and decades of security in front of them, are at stake. So much depends on planning correctly. They cannot make a mistake. If they lose twenty or thirty percent of their assets, they will never recover and their retirement will not be close to what they envisioned.

It's like deciding to climb Mount Everest without a safety line. Nobody would ever consider doing that, but people consider free climbing with their finances all the time in retirement. All their working years, they put money away but never dealt with the market or even followed it – so what makes them think they'll be doing that now? It's not about being a smart guy. It's a matter of the experience and expertise needed to see what could happen.

If you were a leader in your career, you no doubt know how to delegate, how to hire others and tap the shoulder of people who know more than you do about what needs to be done. You were not losing control by delegating. You were taking the reins of leadership, responsibly running the show. Why would it be any different when you're the CEO of your own money?

Copyright 2004 by Randy Glasbergen.
www.glasbergen.com

"They chose those two animals to represent the stock market because your broker will feed you all the bull you can bear."

Whom can you trust?

You may recall the Billy Joel song "Innocent Man," in which he sings, "They will not listen to anyone so nobody tells them a lie." I think that there's a lot to that in the world of financial advice.

As brokers and others have burned investors over the courses of their lifetimes, the investors get to a point where they don't know whom to trust. They come to think that they can only trust themselves to do what's in their best interest with such important decisions.

In determining whom you can trust, I believe you should start by making sure you are working with a fiduciary. This assures you that your best interests financially are being attended to. A fiduciary has a legal liability to do what's in the client's best interest. The stockbroker does not, and the banker does not. The accountant does not. The insurance representative does not.

To find out if you're dealing with a fiduciary, you should ask outright. CFPs, for the most part, are fiduciaries. You can find a CFP by going online to Certified Financial Planners Association. Some of them are not fiduciaries, but that's a place to start. Registered investment advisers also are fiduciaries. If you sign up for a brokerage account and actually read the fine print, you'll see wording indicating that your needs and the needs of the broker are not the same, and if there is a conflict the broker will do what's in the best interest of the company. After the 2008 economic debacle, one Wall Street executive explained why his company shorted investments they had sold to clients – meaning the firm made money only if the investments fell. The clients signed a document, he said, so they should have known their interests weren't the company's.

If you don't like how your money was handled, the company will decide whether the broker was right or wrong – and you can imagine whose side it will take. You'll go to arbitration, which the companies run. I've seen that happen to people many times.

Still, for some reason people think that everybody's looking out for them. That's far from the truth, and in time they learn the hard way. No wonder people are micromanaging. They're scared. But there are steps you can take – and it starts with forming a team to help you.

Assembling a team of experts.

You can think of yourself as the quarterback of your financial team. You're in charge out in the field; you're the one making the calls. Your financial planner is your coach. You also likely will want an attorney on your team, to draft documents, and a certified public accountant.

Your team members need to communicate. How many bad plays do you see in football, where the quarterback throws the ball one way and the receiver runs the other? That's a team that isn't communicating. The members of your financial team are responsible for different aspects of your overall plan, so they need to be in touch so everyone is on the same page.

Often you can defer to your coach – your financial planner – to help you choose the team that's best suited for your needs. If you have a long-standing relationship with an attorney, your planner can work with him or her, but otherwise the planner no doubt has a network of professionals and knows which ones can serve you best in your particular situation.

How often a financial adviser and client should get together depends on the situation.

In the beginning, when I'm preparing the overall plan, I'll meet with a client about once a week for two months to determine the range of what needs to be accomplished and draft strategies toward that end. Once the plan is created and implemented, we meet at least on an annual basis.

Another way to think of your financial planner's role is similar to that of an architect and contractor. If you're building a house, you need an architect to design the overall structure and the layout of the rooms. Once you have that blueprint, then you need a general contractor – and the financial planner plays that role as well, bringing in the people and products needed to complete the job smoothly and expertly. A contractor coordinates the subcontracting of plumbers, electricians and roofers. A financial planner coordinates the attorneys and CPAs and others involved in your strategy.

And once the financial house is built, the planner conducts inspections, quarterly or annually or as needed, depending on how far along the phases have progressed and how much exposure your portfolio has to the elements. A house on the shore that could get pounded by hurricanes needs more attention than one safely tucked away.

An architect, in designing a house, will find some clients with very specific lists of what is to be done, while others will just seem to shrug and defer. My approach to clients is this: "During the planning process, we're going to come to many different decision points, and each time I will tell you the advantages and disadvantage of going either left or right, and I will also tell you the experiences that previous clients have had by going left or right." I'll suggest the client take an action based on previous clients' good results, or I may warn against an action based on troubling results. But at the end of the day, the clients drive the entire process. It's their plan. It's their call.

Everyone wants to do what's best for themselves, so they always choose what they perceive is going to be most advantageous. But there are many times when I'll explain disadvantages and advantages and I'll think that one thing is better, but then the client will explain, "No. I want to do this because I like to keep my money available," or words to that effect. The client has made a reasoned decision to give up a better return in exchange for liquidity. And that, of course, is his prerogative.

How is your adviser compensated?

I can't tell you the number of times people have told me about all the advice a stockbroker has bestowed upon them. "How much is that advice costing you?" I ask. And they say, "Oh, it's not costing me anything. It's free."

They chat with a broker wearing a $2,000 suit in an office that's wall-to-wall mahogany – and they think they're not paying for all that? But that's the way the brokerage world has set things up, so that people don't know what they're really being charged.

When dealing with mutual funds, for example, the brokers call them "B shares" and point out that the client isn't charged a fee to start investing. There is no "load" up front. So the client puts in $100,000 and is pleased to see that amount reflected in the first statement: "Look! There's $100,000 there. They didn't charge me anything."

Front-end loads are obvious. If you invest $100,000 and only $95,000 shows up on the statement, you were charged a five percent load. However, those B shares have what's called a back-end load, meaning investors who pull out early incur a charge of five or six percent. When they get hit with a back-end load when closing out an account, they frequently don't recognize it for what it is. They may presume the market took a dip on the day they sold.

In addition to the back-end load, investors will pay an extra 1.5 to two percent on top of what the internal management fee was going to be. That's basically what the manager gets for handling the fund, and on a typical fund that has been about 1.5 percent. But investors never seem to notice the internal management fee. All they see is their actual performance: "Hey, I was up three percent!" Well, the fund was up six percent, perhaps, but those fees ate up the difference.

Those built-in internal fees can be hard to detect. Brokerage companies don't announce fees in obvious ways. Internal management fees are only disclosed in the prospectus, a thick document of tiny print and a challenge to figure out. You may get the feeling that it was written so you wouldn't be able to understand it even if you consulted it. There has been talk about making them more user-friendly, but ask yourself this: Are the investment houses really motivated to do that for you?

Another charge that a fund investor typically will face is a 12b-1 fee. That is a hidden fee that brings extra compensation to the broker, and it could be 0.5 percent. You also might pay a trading fee and a research fee. Depending on the fund, a variety of charges can be built in, and all you likely will ever notice is how much the fund's value changed, day-to-day or month-to-month. If you want to read about the fees you're paying, you can find them disclosed in the prospectus, in small print, on page 300 or thereabouts.

It all adds up. Perhaps you would have earned ten percent in the market. Let's say your fees are two percent inside. Run the math: If you have $100,000 with a two percent fee over ten years, that costs you $20,000. And that's how they build those big skyscrapers. That's where Wall Street executives get those multimillion-dollar performance bonuses.

As far as dealing with advisers who earn commissions on products, what's important is disclosure. If they're forthright about being paid on commissions, I'm okay with that. I don't want to slam anyone who sells on commission, but doing so is bound to raise questions. Such as: Is the product the best one for the client, or is the adviser's rent due? That conflict may trouble you, even if the adviser's ethics are irreproachable.

A straight fee for service is a fair way to charge clients. If an adviser is charging you a fee, you know exactly what you're paying for. I tell my clients up front exactly what their fee will be. I manage money strictly on a fee of one percent for whatever we're managing, and the only way we get more is if we grow their portfolio.

An adviser who's on your side

I started in my career as a stockbroker. I was in that world. I worked at a brokerage firm for a long time, and it was all about what was generating revenue for the firm. It really had nothing to do with what was in the best interest of the client. If you look at who does all of the advertising on TV, it's Fidelity, it's Vanguard, it's Merrill Lynch, and it's Smith Barney. They're all about accumulation. Their idea of a plan for a senior is to put some assets in really high-risk investments, some in medium risk, and some in low risk. You never hear them say, "Let's put some money aside that isn't subjected to risk at all." They don't get paid for that. They get paid to manage risk.

When I was a stockbroker, I could see the prevailing philosophy of a lot of money managers: "We've got to grow the assets." What does it profit them for a retiree to have money set aside that's safe? They do, however, recognize that retirees are attracted to such talk.

For example, a lot of brokers will put retired clients in a product that's called a variable annuity. They sell it as if it were some kind of guaranteed product. I see these all the time, with various bells and whistles. "It's guaranteed," people declare of their variable annuities. What they don't realize is that when the broker told them it was guaranteed, the only guarantee associated with it is when they die. Their heirs will receive the highest amount the annuity ever attained. But that doesn't do retirees any good if they need it for income during their lifetime.

However the variable annuity world does offer income riders. For a fee of one or two percent, you can get a guaranteed increase in account value – a guaranteed growth as high as six percent. The trap is that there is no way to get access to that as a lump sum withdrawal. The only way to get access to that guaranteed growth is to agree to a lifetime income, ranging from three to seven percent of the balance per year, based on your age. Though this could be beneficial, the buyer must be very educated about all of the rules.

With a variable annuity, basically what happens is you give your money to the stockbroker, and the stockbroker gives your money to an insurance company, and the insurance company gives it to an investment company. The investment company takes a fee, and the insurance company takes a fee, and the broker takes a fee. You'll be looking at three to five percent in fees on these things.

Everyone's smiling, including, unfortunately, the retiree. The retiree could have gone directly to a mutual fund company for half or a third of the fees and had better performance – and without any real difference in risk. Yet retirees buy this product, and it's only because of the way it is sold. It may not be appropriate for them.

At your age, if you need a doctor, do you go to a pediatrician? No, you're likely to go to a gerontologist, someone with more appropriate knowledge of what your needs are likely to be. It's similar with your financial health. A stockbroker helps people accumulate assets. But a retiree can't afford to be taking that kind of risk. I think that people who work with a broker in retirement are being foolish with their money. They're taking more risk than they need to.

The lesson bears repeating: Go with an adviser who keeps your interests in mind. If you do, you can be confident you'll be retiring on your own terms – not somebody else's.

What's in Your Buckets?

"What's the matter, girl? Is Timmy's portfolio in trouble?"

Once you get to retirement, you have to start looking at assets differently. If you keep your nest egg in the traditional asset allocation model – that big pile of money in the sky – you're going to take financial hits. We all know the market's going to go down at times, whether tomorrow or next year, and if you keep everything at various levels of risk, a single down year during your retirement can flatten your fortunes forever.

Bucket planning is a different way of looking at your assets. Let's take a closer look at this concept. It can change your life.

During the accumulation years, people look at their assets as being in that one pile. They have assets in growth investments of various sorts. A million-dollar portfolio, for example, might have 20 percent in large cap, 20 percent in small cap, 20 percent in bonds, 20 percent in international, and so on. Such is the asset allocation strategy.

The concept of that common strategy is simply that if the market goes bad, some of the assets will stay afloat. That's actually okay during the accumulation years because you're not drawing income off of those assets. The markets rebound, as markets do. That comfortable salary you're earning means you don't need to touch those assets for income, and you can afford the time for their recovery.

Bucket planning, by contrast, is designed to give you money you can depend on for the short term, to spend right away in your retirement, while also looking out for your needs in the years ahead.

The concept, in essence, involves allocating money for when you'll actually need it as income. It uses the same math that bankers love and puts it to work in your favor. It's beautifully simple. Remember the truth-in-lending form you received when you bought your last house? It informed you that you weren't actually going to pay the $500,000 price. You were going to pay more like $1.5

million for that house, once you paid the interest over the term of the mortgage. That's how much the bankers gained through the principal of compounding interest.

Bucket planning works the same way, except that the interest compounds in your favor. First you gain, and then you can gain on your gains. Let's see how you can do it.

First, let's look at all your assets and separate it into categories, or buckets, of income money and growth money. The income money will be what you think you'll need to spend in the next several years. That could be a range of five to twenty years, depending on how much you have in assets and how much risk you'll need to take to meet your goals. All that can be calculated.

Let's say we figure your income needs for ten years and set that much money aside. We put that money into investments that will provide you the income that you will need, right when you need it.

The remainder of your portfolio, then, will represent money that you know you won't need for at least ten years. That's your growth money. That's the bucket of money that you can expose to risk to grow in the markets, and if you take a hit, you'll have ten years to recover.

In this strategy, we label several buckets. We call them Buckets A, B, and C, and then we skip to Bucket G. There are several buckets that we sometimes use in between C and G, but those we reserve for individualizing specific accounts.

Bucket A is for the income you'll need for the first five years of retirement. It earns little, but the money is liquid and accessible.

Buckets B, C and G are reserved for use in your later years. Those three buckets have higher earnings, and the money is left in them to compound. Bucket B is the income for the second five years of your retirement. Bucket C is the income for years eleven through twenty. Bucket G is money that you allow to be exposed to market risk.

Bucket A: Your income bucket

Bucket A is simply a distribution bucket. The sole purpose of Bucket A is to make sure that over the next five years, you have the income that you need and want. So Bucket A is in a very low-earning account, typically, and that can be anything from a personal pension to a savings account to CDs or other options. The money needs to be liquid. Almost everybody I've ever worked with takes money in retirement on a monthly basis, and so they need the ability to be able to draw money from a guaranteed source on a monthly basis for the next five years.

Why five years? When I first began setting up this system, I tried using a one-year bucket. It got too complicated. People with twenty or thirty years of retirement in front of them were trying to balance far too many buckets to feel comfortable. I also have considered a ten-year time period for the early buckets, but that was simply too long for sufficient flexibility. Five is just right.

So for those first five years, we find the best rate we can for an accessible account where you will have no trouble getting at it. This bucket has two overriding criteria: Most important is guaranteed principal, and second is availability. It must be safe and there for you when you need it. The interest rate is another factor to consider, of course, but in this bucket one would choose a zero percent return with guaranteed principal over, say, a five percent return with risk. We just simply won't take any risk in Bucket A. If you need the money, you need the money. You don't want to worry what the stock market's doing.

Bucket A, therefore, is your lowest earning account. You'll be getting half a percent in interest on that money, if you're lucky. But it comes without strings attached. You can pull the money out easily, without consequence. During the course of those five years, you empty that bucket, without touching any of the other ones, where your money is earning perhaps four or five percent. This is where the math really starts to work for you.

Think of it as the economic principle of opportunity cost. If you pull the income you need from Bucket A, where the interest rate is the lowest, you are enhancing your opportunity for gain in those higher-earning buckets. Most people want to do the opposite: They take money from higher-earning accounts, believing they've done well if the account quickly recovers. But look at the opportunity lost. They could have left that money alone to compound at an auspicious rate. Instead, they fetch zero. They could have drawn the income instead from a lower-earning account, where they would not have suffered the loss of compounding power.

In short, by drawing money from your lowest-earning account, you allow your higher-earning accounts to compound. And the compounding on those accounts, if we set up our buckets correctly, is usually enough to cover the amount of money that you withdraw. For example, if you will be taking out $20,000 a year from Bucket A, your bucket strategy will be designed so that Buckets B, C and G compound sufficiently so that your assets keep growing nonetheless.

How much in each bucket?

In the example on the following pages, we have used the hypothetical rates of two percent for bucket A, five percent for Bucket B, six percent for Bucket C, and seven percent for Bucket G. In 2012 we are using much lower rates than those for each bucket, and the plans still work. As interest rates rise, each of these buckets will look even better.

How do you determine the percentage of the total portfolio that goes into Bucket A, your low-interest, very liquid account? First I look at the client's age and total liquid assets. Then, based on those figures, I can calculate the maximum amount of income possible the first year, and then grow that income for each of the ensuing four years to stay ahead of inflation. That same calculation is used to determine how much is set aside for the other buckets, B, C and G, which earn higher rates but won't be available until years down the road.

It's part art and part science, but here's how it works: The very first time I sit down with a client to go through this, I come up with a total for their liquid investable assets, not counting real estate. We take that number and run a distribution plan out to age one hundred. I always start with that age, because I think it's a safe place to start with life expectancies right now. We can have the client die sooner, if he wants – on paper, that is. But I suggest that everyone plan to age one hundred.

Then it's simply a calculation to figure out how much income they can draw from that asset at those varying interest rates so that at age one hundred they have exactly zero left.

That's how it's set up the first time I run the figures. "Yes, let's do it that way," clients sometimes say. "I want my assets to run out when I die. I want the most income while I'm alive." So I figure the maximum amount of income to leave the client without assets at age one hundred.

The next question, of course, is: Will that be enough income? If the client says, "That's more than I need," we

Steve & Sally Sample

Emergency Cash		$50,000					

#1	#2		#3	#4	#5	#6	#7	#8
Year	Age			Total income	Pension	Social Security		Income from Assets
	Assumed Rate					2%	2%	
1	66	69	2007	$120,000	$24,824	$21,396	$13,264	$60,516
2	67	70	2008	$120,693	$24,824	$21,824	$13,529	$60,516
3	68	71	2009	$121,400	$24,824	$22,260	$13,800	$60,516
4	69	72	2010	$122,121	$24,824	$22,706	$14,076	$60,516
5	70	73	2011	$122,857	$24,824	$23,160	$14,357	$60,516
6	71	74	2012	$132,685	$24,824	$23,623	$14,645	$69,593
7	72	75	2013	$133,450	$24,824	$24,095	$14,937	$69,593
8	73	76	2014	$134,231	$24,824	$24,577	$15,236	$69,593
9	74	77	2015	$135,027	$24,824	$25,069	$15,541	$69,593
10	75	78	2016	$135,839	$24,824	$25,570	$15,852	$69,593
11	76	79	2017	$147,107	$24,824	$26,082	$16,169	$80,032
12	77	80	2018	$147,952	$24,824	$26,603	$16,492	$80,032
13	78	81	2019	$148,814	$24,824	$27,135	$16,822	$80,032
14	79	82	2020	$149,693	$24,824	$27,678	$17,158	$80,032
15	80	83	2021	$150,590	$24,824	$28,232	$17,502	$80,032
16	81	84	2022	$163,509	$24,824	$28,796	$17,852	$92,037
17	82	85	2023	$164,442	$24,824	$29,372	$18,209	$92,037
18	83	86	2024	$165,394	$24,824	$29,960	$18,573	$92,037
19	84	87	2025	$166,364	$24,824	$30,559	$18,944	$92,037
20	85	88	2026	$167,354	$24,824	$31,170	$19,323	$92,037
21	86	89	2027	$182,170	$24,824	$31,793	$19,710	$105,843
22	87	90	2028	$183,200	$24,824	$32,429	$20,104	$105,843
23	88	91	2029	$184,251	$24,824	$33,078	$20,506	$105,843
24	89	92	2030	$185,322	$24,824	$33,739	$20,916	$105,843
25	90	93	2031	$186,415	$24,824	$34,414	$21,334	$105,843
26	91	94	2032	$206,582	$24,824	$35,102	$21,761	$124,895
27	92	95	2033	$207,719	$24,824	$35,804	$22,196	$124,895
28	93	96	2034	$208,879	$24,824	$36,521	$22,640	$124,895
29	94	97	2035	$210,062	$24,824	$37,251	$23,093	$124,895
30	95	98	2036	$211,269	$24,824	$37,996	$23,555	$124,895
31	96	99	2037	$234,981	$24,824	$38,756	$24,026	$147,376
32	97	100	2038	$236,237	$24,824	$39,531	$24,506	$147,376
33	98		2039	$237,518	$24,824	$40,322	$24,997	$147,376
34	99		2040	$238,824	$24,824	$41,128	$25,496	$147,376
35	100		2041	$240,157	$24,824	$41,951	$26,006	$147,376

Hypothetical Example:
No specific investments portrayed

#9	#10	#11	#12	#13	#14
Cumulative Income from Assets	Bucket A	Bucket B	Bucket C	Bucket G	Projected Account Balance W/ Cash
	2%	5%	6%	7%	
$60,516	$289,830	$270,147	$445,806	$693,874	$1,749,656
$121,032	$175,132	$284,735	$474,337	$745,221	$1,729,424
$181,548	$118,443	$300,110	$504,695	$800,367	$1,773,616
$242,064	$60,516	$316,316	$536,995	$859,594	$1,823,422
$302,580	-$0	$333,398	$571,363	$923,204	$1,877,964
$372,173	$269,570		$607,930	$991,521	$1,919,021
$441,767	$204,347		$646,838	$1,064,894	$1,966,078
$511,360	$137,698		$688,235	$1,143,696	$2,019,629
$580,954	$69,593		$732,282	$1,228,329	$2,080,205
$650,547	$0		$779,148	$1,319,226	$2,148,374
$730,579	$714,395			$1,416,848	$2,181,244
$810,612	$648,227			$1,521,695	$2,219,922
$890,644	$580,613			$1,634,300	$2,264,913
$970,677	$511,520			$1,755,239	$2,316,759
$1,050,709	$440,918			$1,885,126	$2,376,045
$1,142,746	$356,506			$2,024,626	$2,431,132
$1,234,784	$270,249			$2,174,448	$2,494,697
$1,326,821	$182,106			$2,335,357	$2,567,463
$1,418,858	$92,037			$2,508,174	$2,650,211
$1,510,895	$0			$2,693,778	$2,743,778
$1,616,738	$105,843			$2,733,400	$2,889,242
$1,722,581	$105,843			$2,775,160	$2,931,003
$1,828,424	$105,843			$2,819,176	$2,975,019
$1,934,267	$105,843			$2,865,569	$3,021,412
$2,040,110	$105,843			$2,914,467	$3,070,310
$2,165,004	$124,895			$2,946,953	$3,121,848
$2,289,899	$124,895			$2,981,194	$3,156,089
$2,414,793	$124,895			$3,017,284	$3,192,179
$2,539,688	$124,895			$3,055,323	$3,230,217
$2,664,583	$124,895			$3,095,416	$3,270,310
$2,811,958	$147,376			$3,115,193	$3,312,568
$2,959,334	$147,376			$3,136,037	$3,333,413
$3,106,709	$147,376			$3,158,008	$3,355,383
$3,254,085	$147,376			$3,181,165	$3,378,540
$3,401,461	$147,376			$3,205,572	$3,402,947

3% Inflation

111

make adjustments and plan to leave money for heirs. If the client says it's not enough, then we go to an advanced planning stage, in which we can't be quite as conservative.

The chart on the previous page is a hypothetical example, and does not reflect any actual investments. Once this chart has been finalized for a client, we look at what options exist and add them to the chart. Depending on interest rates at the time, the projected rates will be increased or decreased according to what is available. If rates are lower than what we represented in this chart, we simply add more money at the top and less if rates are higher. Rates will affect the actual amount of income a client will receive, but they will know that during the planning phase and not be surprised by that realization somewhere down the road. Looking at the chart, you can see the distribution of a retirement account that started with $1.75 million. You will see that the income increases every year. Column #8 is the one that has assets producing income. Every five years, all the way to age one hundred, the amount in that column increases.

For clients who tell me they need more income up front, I run the figures to give them the bulk of their money up through about their early eighties, and then I actually decrease their income. That reflects those typical "go-go" to "slow go" to "no-go" phases of retirement – when they start to slow down, they simply won't be spending as much money. Then when they get into their nineties, I'll decrease their income again. That makes the up-front income significantly higher. That's part of the planning process. That's about creating the cash flow that they need. If I can create a bucket plan where I don't need to do that, I won't.

"Is it better to invest during a bull market or bear market?
Depends...would you rather be gored or mauled?"

Buckets B, C and G: The growth buckets

Once you have put all the income you'll need for those first five years into Bucket A, you can comfortably set aside your remaining assets for later use, knowing you won't have to touch them for years. You'll put that money in Buckets B, C and G. You can get a better rate of return on your investments with this money. What you'll lose is liquidity.

You won't have immediate access to these accounts. You won't need it.

In the chart, you can see that Bucket B is paying five percent. That will vary depending on the prevailing interest rates, but the system still works even in a near-zero rate environment. We find some instrument out there that will provide the higher return, even though it won't be liquid for five years. In the meantime, of course, you're using up your Bucket A.

Ideally Buckets A, B, and C, are all in guaranteed principal accounts. When possible only Bucket G should have risk. This will provide a much more stable and predictable income.

We know we don't need Bucket B's funds for five years, so it grows for that time. Then, at the end of five years, we move it over to a liquid account. It becomes the new Bucket A, on which you draw for income in the ensuing five years – the sixth through tenth years of retirement.

Notice the income increases from the first five years to the second five years. We project the inflation rate – say, three percent annually. We don't actually increase the figures every year, but rather every five years – so, in that example, the income goes up 15 percent to start each five-year period.

So Bucket B provides the income money for the second five-year period of retirement. At the end of the tenth year, as you can see in the chart, the cumulative income from assets is $650,547. That's how much the retiree has taken from the original $1.75 million, and it does not include income from pensions or Social Security.

That's about thirty percent of what he started with. People get a little nervous when I say that. But if you look over to the far right, even though the retiree has taken that thirty percent, you'll notice that the figure in column #14 has actually increased significantly. So even though the retiree has taken so much money out, the account total has still grown. That's the benefit of compounding interest. At some point, as the retiree ages, the bucket chart will begin to show total assets decreasing year to year. Most people want to spend their assets during their lifetimes.

Now, at the end of the tenth year, Bucket C becomes available for income use, as arranged when we set up the plan. We had Bucket A for the first five years and Bucket B for the second five. And once again, we were able to get a better rate on the money in Bucket C by having it set aside for a longer period of time – in this case, ten years. Wherever we could get the best ten-year rate is where we invested that money. And for ten years, it grew undisturbed.

The chart shows Bucket C growing at six percent, as an example. And that's still an investment that is not risky. The principle is guaranteed – whether it's a bank CD or an annuity or a bond or similar vehicle.

The buckets, then, shift with the passing of the years. When Bucket A is gone, Bucket B takes its place and is renamed, and Bucket C moves over to take Bucket B's place. That leaves us with the need to create a new Bucket C, however, which will be designated for use ten or fifteen years in the future.

Where does the money come from for the new bucket? We can pull it from Bucket G, in which we have placed money at risk in the markets. However, you now have time on your side in deciding when to do so. Even though you're retired, you can think like a young investor because you're dealing with money not to be touched for many years. So if the market tumbles, that's no time to withdraw the money from the falling Bucket G. It can be left there untouched to recover, and when it does, that's when we can create your new Bucket C.

The results of this planning method are impressive — and it's based on what seems like the magic of the compounding return, the same principle that pays the bank so handsomely when you send in your mortgage. On the chart, look at the bottom of column #9 to see how much the assets totaled at year one hundred: You'll see it's $3.401 million. That's based on a modest rate of return in the various asset classes. This particular retiree started with $1.75 million, took an income of $3.4 million, and still had about $3.4 million left to leave to heirs. The retiree didn't expect to spend more — which just meant we had to do some estate planning as well, hardly a bad outcome.

Which assets are right for each bucket?

In addition to setting up the buckets, we evaluate all potential investments to determine in which bucket, if any, they would be appropriate. We look at all the asset classes available. We look at how each investment works and what it is capable of doing.

As you can see in the chart on page 119, the legend across the top lists eight options, columns A through H. Each is an attribute that an investment might offer. Column A is monthly income, column B is guaranteed principal, column C tax deferral, D is a fixed rate, E is an upside market potential, F is no annual fees, G is no fees to purchase, and H is liquidity. (I leave a space for other possible investment categories, but it's been a few years since a client has suggested we add anything – so I think it's pretty detailed at this point.)

Down the left-hand side is a list of potential invest-ments, each of them rated for those eight options. They are either appropriate or inappropriate for the bucket being considered – thus, the smiley and frowny face symbols.

As far as specific investment advice on which you should choose for your own buckets, every retiree's situation is different and needs to be sized up with pro-fessional counsel. A financial adviser can help you guide your decisions so your investments are appropriate for your portfolio and advance your life goals. However, this chart will show you the criteria for which type of investments work best in which buckets. It explores the universe of investment categories that could be at your disposal.

Let's look at Bucket A. I only have two requirements for an investment in Bucket A. It has to have either the ability to generate monthly income, or it must have a guaranteed principal. If it doesn't have one of those, which are the first two columns, it doesn't qualify as even a possibility in Bucket A. For example, commodities would never be appropriate for Bucket A.

The chart, then, shows how specific investments, listed down the left side, would serve you for each of the considerations listed along the top. Municipal bonds, for example, lack a monthly income, so they get a frown for that attribute. However, they do have guaranteed principal, so for that attribute they get a smile. We go through all of the options. Then I work with the client to decide which ones are appropriate for his or her particular situation and which have the best rates. We narrow it down to two or three choices.

Legend			
A	Monthly Income	E	Upside Market Potential
B	Guaranteed Principal	F	NO Annual Fees
C	Tax Deferral	G	NO Fees to Purchase
D	Fixed Rate	H	Liquidity

	A	B	C	D	E	F	G	H
Municipal Bonds	☹	☺	☺	☺	☹	☺	☹	☹
Corporate Bonds	☹	☺	☹	☺	☹	☺	☹	☹
Utility Bonds	☹	☺	☹	☺	☹	☺	☹	☹
Government Securities	☹	☺	☹	☺	☹	☺	☹	☹
Certificate of Deposit	☹	☺	☹	☺	☹	☺	☺	☺
Fixed Annuities	☹	☺	☺	☺	☹	☺	☺	☺
Equity Indexed Account	☹	☺	☺	☺	☺	☺	☺	☺
Savings Account	☺	☺	☹	☺	☹	☺	☺	☺
Personal Pension	☺	☺	☺	☺	☹	☺	☺	☺
Life Insurance	☺	☺	☺	☺	☺	☹	☺	☺
Variable Annuities	☺	☹	☺	☹	☺	☹	☺	☹
Real Estate	☺	☹	☹	☹	☺	☹	☹	☹
Mutual Funds	☺	☹	☹	☹	☺	☹	☹	☹
Bond Funds	☺	☹	☹	☹	☺	☹	☹	☹
Commodities	☹	☹	☹	☹	☺	☺	☹	☹
Futures	☹	☹	☹	☹	☺	☺	☹	☹
Foreign Exchange	☹	☹	☹	☹	☺	☺	☹	☹
Stocks	☹	☹	☹	☹	☺	☺	☹	☹
Oil & Gas Partnership	☹	☹	☹	☹	☺	☹	☹	☹
ETF's	☹	☹	☹	☹	☺	☹	☹	☹
	A	B	C	D	E	F	G	H

Notice that investments such as variable annuities, real estate, mutual funds, and bonds all have a frowny face for guaranteed principal, or column B. Still, they are on the list because they do have a smiley face for Column A, or monthly income. In that way, they meet minimum criteria, but that doesn't mean they would be appropriate for a particular client. In fact, using one of those options in Bucket A violates one of my basic rules of planning: Never, ever draw income from a fluctuating account. I am often asked why those options are listed there at all if they violate the rules. The reason is that each individual's situation and assets are different. I want to make sure we evaluate them on their merits. Having said that, it would have to be a highly unusual situation to ever consider using any investment without a guaranteed principal as an income option in Bucket A.

Also note that Buckets B, C and G carry no restrictions on what could be available – and that's why the sheets for those buckets are exactly the same. We're talking about the same investments, but what may be appropriate for B is not appropriate for C, and so on. And what's appropriate for G certainly isn't appropriate for B.

We still want to follow the guidelines for what each bucket is intended to accomplish. Looking at Bucket B, we said we ideally want a guaranteed principal account. So as we go down the list of investments, I will draw a line under "personal pensions." Everything above personal pensions has a guaranteed principal. Everything below personal pensions does not have a guaranteed principal. In an ideal world, we'd want to restrict Buckets B and C to investments above that line.

Now, if we have to take on risk to get what we need for retirement income, then we purposefully cross that line and understand that we're adding risk. People will say, "Oh well, my mutual funds are safe." Well, they might be safe, but they're not a guaranteed principal. They might choose to accept that risk, but they need to understand and acknowledge it.

A lot of people think success requires more risk than it truly does. The reality is that taking that risk can decrease chances of success. You can have more money, less volatility, and more peace of mind without adding any risk or increasing rates in any way. You can feel confident that you will have the income that you need and want for the rest of your life.

It's About Living Well

LOANS

"Do you have any other collateral...
besides this e-mail from a Nigerian prince?"

"T he days all seem pretty much the same, whether it's Tuesday or Saturday," a retired friend told me, and then he launched into a story. One evening at a restaurant, he and his wife were surprised when the maître d' told them they would have to wait forty-five minutes – but it was, after all, a weekend, which they hadn't realized. "Son," he told the maître d', "my wife and I are both in our nineties. We may not have forty-five minutes." They were seated immediately. He made the same comment at another restaurant when faced with a long wait, and again they were seated at once. He uses that line regularly now.

And why not? As a retiree, you've worked hard for a few extras. You should be doing what you want to do, the things you dreamed about doing. If you work, it should be because that's your desire. You shouldn't feel thwarted by financial pressures – either real ones because you truly didn't plan properly, or imagined ones because you lack the proper guidance to reassure you that you'll actually be all right.

In this book, I have offered you guidance in your financial planning that can lead to peace of mind through-out your retirement. The definition of wealth today is all about income – you need not take the risks that you may have thought you should take. In fact, taking those risks could ruin you financially.

You'll be able to sleep well, knowing you'll have a good income through the simple principal of compound interest. It has been called the eighth wonder of the world. It works for bankers. It can work for you.

It can work, that is, if you take action. To paraphrase an old Chinese proverb: "To know and not to do is not to know." For most of the retirees whom I deal with, I have found that unless they're in the grip of a burning issue, they don't really get it. They don't find the time to act. They tell me all the time that they're busier than ever. I'm reminded again of my father's words: "I wake up in the morning with nothing to do, and I go to bed with it half done."

Retirees either don't know where to start and what to do, or they have so many other plans and responsibilities that seem more pressing to them. They don't pay enough attention to their finances until they're in crisis mode.

Though they are uniformly concerned about having enough income for the rest of their lives, very few retirees know where to go for answers. Often they go to stockbrokers, who are unlikely to dispense the advice that will serve them best. A stockbroker's tack might be a good one for a young investor. For a retiree, it can cause a financial fatality.

Fear and procrastination can steal a retiree's dreams away as surely as investment mistakes. One thing that I typically will tell clients when they engage my firm is that they're finally out of harm's way. They're financially secure. Once they retire, the time for taking chances is over – and many times, the financial planning we do together is the only thing that stands between them and the prospects of a catastrophic loss. Yet a staggering number of retirees don't seek out such planning.

I have no idea what's going to happen in the market in the next ten years. I don't even know what the market's going to do today. In fact, I would argue, anybody who's predicting the market is selling something to you, something not necessarily best for you. It well could be what's best for the seller.

Still, when the market took the worst beating in our experience recently, down forty percent, none of my clients had to change anything about their lives. They didn't have to curtail the things that they were doing. They may have lost money in the market, but nothing about their income changed. The money they needed for expenses was in accounts that were unfazed, and any assets exposed to market risk could be left untouched to recover. That speaks volumes about how well our planning method works. It's quite reassuring.

Such reassurance means you don't have to be glued to the TV and listening to those talking heads, each of whom has some angle. You need not worry and fret. That's not what retirement should be about. You've had enough stress in your career; why trade it for even more? You can have fun with the grandkids. You might go to see Paris.

I see retirees in the full range of financial conditions. One came into my office recently, unable to retire. He had attended one of our seminars a few years earlier, but he had decided to just wait a bit before taking action. Along came the crash, and he wasn't protected. Had he only come to see me earlier, we could have done so much to dramatically improve his situation.

And I also see clients such as the couple who came in recently, figuring they could manage, somehow, to get by on $25,000 a year beyond the pensions that each of them had – a rarity these days – and their Social Security. That's the most they figured they could withdraw annually from their assets without becoming paupers. I ran their figures.

"Listen," I told them, "you can actually spend up to $60,000 a year and not worry about running out of money before you die."

"No," they responded, almost in unison. "We could never do that. That's way too extravagant for us." And that, of course, was their choice to make. Clients pay me for my advice; they certainly don't have to take it.

However, I knew that their three children were coming home for the holidays, so I asked if we could invite them to come to the office, too, and talk about the situation. When they did, I explained the same scenario, the $25,000 vs. the $60,000.

"Come on, Mom, Dad – we're doing fine," they said, as we sat around the conference table. "You deserve to enjoy your money." So their parents relented. Did they spend it? No. What they did instead was to start making gifts to the children and grandchildren – something they otherwise never would have done, for fear of running out.

And last Christmas, that couple took their entire family – children and grandchildren – on a weeklong Caribbean cruise. They created memories that the whole family, young and old, will carry for their lifetimes. Careful planning, and the reassurance that can result from it, made it possible.

That's what it's all about. This book may sometimes have seemed to be all about figures, and money buckets, and investment tools. Those are important, indeed. But it's also about memories, and living well – as well as you possibly can for the rest of your life, without worries, knowing that you are in safe hands. If you take the information I have given you in this book, and truly follow it, or come see me and I will help you do it, you will be well on your way to living happily ever after.

**INVESTMENTS AND
FINANCIAL PLANNING**

GLASBERGEN

**"I retire on Friday and I haven't saved a dime.
Here's your chance to become a legend!"**

A founding partner of Absolute Return Solutions, based in Redmond, Washington, Jim Black has twenty-five years of experience in all aspects of financial and tax strategy planning. A graduate of Brigham Young University with a degree in international finance, Black earned his MBA from Willamette University.

As a certified financial planner (CFP), his focus has become distribution planning, helping clients who are fifty-five and over, or those who expect to retire within five years, to move forward on their own terms. He works with them to preserve assets while striving to assure a dependable income that will last a lifetime.

"The change in focus," he says, "resulted from observing that what worked for clients before retirement wasn't really working for them during retirement. Their needs called for a different approach. Once they received the last employee paycheck they were ever going to get (for the rest of their lives), things changed, but they didn't get a new set of rules or a new way of looking at things.

"Cash flow is king in retirement," Black explains, "yet for most money managers, everything's about growing that portfolio. In reality, you can have $10 million in assets, but if you don't have a liquid income and can't pay the electric bill, you aren't going to be very happy. You need more than growth of your portfolio during those twenty or thirty years of retirement; you also need income, regularly and consistently."

The wrong approach, he warns, has cost people their retirement dreams. In the recent downturn, some people lost as much as 70 or 80 percent of their portfolios because they violated a basic rule of retirement: Never draw income from a fluctuating account, such as mutual funds, stocks, or bonds. "Nevertheless, that's what they did," Black says, "and that's what the brokerage world continues to tell everybody to do."

Because he is an independent financial planner, Black can objectively advise and help to choose services that best serve clients' needs and strategies, along with providing supporting research. His goal is to free retirees to enjoy their lives without stress.

Contact:

Absolute Return Solutions
18300 Redmond Way, Ste. 100
Redmond, WA 98052

Phone (425) 558-3700
Email info@absolutereturnsolutions.com

Printed in the USA
CPSIA information can be obtained
at www.ICGtesting.com
JSHW082214140824
68134JS00014B/625